BRIGGS & STRATTON

Outdoor Cleaning with
PRESSURE WASHERS

Creative Publishing
international

CHANHASSEN, MINNESOTA
www.creativepub.com

Outdoor Cleaning with Pressure Washers

Created by: Creative Publishing international, Inc.,
in cooperation with Briggs & Stratton Corporation.

Post Office Box 702
Milwaukee, WI 53201-0702
1-800-233-3723
www.briggsandstratton.com
www.tuneupmonth.com

Vice President, Marketing: William Reitman
Marketing Director: Scott Alderton
Marketing Manager: Steve Kruger
Manager of Service Marketing: Cherie Burns-Boldt
Technical Editors: Carl Jahns, Rick Gilpatrick, Mark Warnke
Marketing Coordinators: Jen Christianson, Scott Deibel, Synoilva Shaw
Image Studios, John Neinhaus Photography, Allen Knox Studios

Creative Publishing international

18705 Lake Drive East
Chanhassen, MN 55317
1-800-328-3895
www.creativepub.com

President: Ken Fund
Vice President, Publisher: Linda Ball
Vice President, Retail Sales: Kevin Haas
Executive Editor: Bryan Trandem

Author: Thomas Lemmer
Managing Editor: Michelle Skudlarek
Copy Editors: Janice Cauley, Lisa Lupo
Art Directors: Kari Johnston, Jim Oldsberg
Mac Production Artist: Dave McCullough
Project Manager: Christy Balfanz
Production Managers: Helga Thielen, Stacy Vergin
Director Production Services & Photography: Kim Gerber
Studio Services Manager: Jeanette Moss McCurdy
Lead Photographer: Tate Carlson
Photographers: Andrea Rugg, Joel Schnell, Stanley Leary Photography
Photo Technician & Set Design: Randy Austin

A special thanks to the following people and companies:
Patio Town, patiotown.com, 1-800-770-4525
Tom, Peggy, and Eric Rice
Jim and Christa Oldsberg
Jim and Jan Oldsberg
Pat Simpson, Before and After

Library of Congress
Cataloging-in-Publication Data
(Information on file)
ISBN 1-58923-166-X

Pat Simpson has been building and designing for over 20 years. With the experience gained from erecting houses, lake homes, and other structures with his father and friends, Pat has become a regular contributor to a number of consumer and trade publications. He is a much sought-after speaker for media tours, home shows, and home center grand openings, as well as the spokesperson for a variety of national home improvement manufacturers. Currently, Pat can be seen on The Home & Garden Network (HGTV) as the host of three hit programs: *Room to Improve, Before & After* and *Fix It Up!*

Briggs & Stratton's Edge

Briggs & Stratton has almost 100 years' experience in manufacturing outdoor power equipment for consumers worldwide. This quintessential American company is also a major producer of four-stroke, small engines for almost every application. You may find many brands of pressure washers, mowers, and other equipment at your power equipment retailer, but look closely: chances are good that the engines are built by Briggs & Stratton. Retailers often point this out, because the Briggs & Stratton name stands for quality and experience.

You can rest assured that the detailed information and thorough instructions collected in *Outdoor Cleaning with Pressure Washers* provides all the skill and know-how you need to get the most out of your pressure washer and keep your home looking beautiful for years.

Table of Contents

Cleaning Projects (continued)

INTRODUCTION

Pressure washers are transforming the way we clean and maintain our property.

A weathered deck, mud-covered truck, or oil-stained driveway can be restored to like-new condition in a fraction of the time when cleaned by pressure washer rather than by hand.

Outdoor Cleaning with Pressure Washers is filled with information to help you safely operate, properly maintain, and effectively use your pressure washer. This book contains detailed descriptions and straightforward instructions with more than 300 full-color photographs and illustrations. It is arranged into four main sections, allowing you to quickly and easily locate the specific information you want:

Getting to Know Your Pressure Washer

The first section of the book discusses the function and performance of your pressure washer and its attachments. Here you will learn about the basic pressure washer machine and components and how the system produces the high-pressure water spray that cleans your outdoor surfaces faster and more effectively than any other cleaning method. The standard parts (high-pressure hoses, spray wands, and nozzles) and a variety of specialty attachments are described in detail, as are the various types of cleaning detergents and maintenance products available to help you get the most out of your pressure washer.

This section also explains how PSI (pounds per square inch), GPM (gallons per minute), and the distance between the nozzle and the cleaning surface all factor into the effectiveness of a pressure washer's cleaning power.

Basic Operation & Techniques

In the second section you will find detailed instructions to guide you through the assembly, operation, and basic pressure washing process. Each step of the action is given special attention, from hooking up the water supply and high-pressure hose to using cleaning detergents and specialty attachments. A variety of general pressure washing techniques are included to help you achieve the best results when cleaning any outdoor surface.

In addition, this section will teach you the most important pressure washing technique—adjusting the cleaning power. By simply testing the effectiveness of the nozzle spray on the cleaning surface, you will be able to determine the most appropriate spray patterns and pressure settings for faster, more effective pressure washing of your outdoor surfaces.

Cleaning Projects

The third section illustrates how those once daunting outdoor cleaning chores become simple tasks with the aid of a pressure washer. Each of the nine chapters in this section contains information on site preparation, safety tips, and project-specific cleaning techniques, along with step-by-step sequences to take you through many pressure washing projects.

Chapters Include:
- Housing Exteriors
- Decks & Fences
- Driveways, Sidewalks & Patios
- Vehicles & Boats
- Stripping Paint
- And more!

This section also includes a Portfolio of before-and-after photographs to demonstrate the effectiveness of pressure washing versus traditional cleaning methods; and Pat Simpson Pro Tips, which offer advanced techniques and creative uses for your pressure washer.

Maintenance & Storage

The fourth and final section of the book outlines a number of important precautions, maintenance tips, and minor repairs to help ensure your pressure washer performs at its peak for years to come. You also will find information on long-term storage requirements, such as water pump protection and small engine care.

In the last few pages you will find a wealth of references and resources related to maintaining, repairing, and better understanding your pressure washer:

- Troubleshooting Guide helps you identify and correct common operational and mechanical problems you may encounter while using your pressure washer.
- Shopper's Guide provides information on locating Briggs & Stratton dealers in your area.
- Resources List contains information on pressure washer-related associations, publications, and websites that can help further your knowledge and understanding of pressure washers.

As you can see, Briggs & Stratton's *Outdoor Cleaning with Pressure Washers* is a practical guide for operating, using, and maintaining your pressure washer. Use it to help make all of your outdoor cleaning projects faster, easier, and more fun!

GETTING TO KNOW YOUR PRESSURE WASHER

GETTING TO KNOW YOUR PRESSURE WASHER

To clean the surfaces and objects around the outside of your home, there is nothing that works faster or more effectively than a pressure washer. A typical residential-grade unit can be as much as 50 times more powerful than a standard garden hose, while using up to 80% less water. To take advantage of this cleaning power, it is helpful to know how the machine and its components work.

A pressure washer is comprised of an engine to generate power, a pump to force water supplied from a garden hose through a high-pressure hose, and a nozzle to accelerate the water stream leaving the system. This results in a high-pressure water jet ranging from 500 to 4000 PSI (pounds per square inch).

Although a pressure washer's water pump rating is generally based on its maximum water-pressure setting, the unit's water-flow output, or GPM (gallons per minute), is just as important. Ultimately, it is the combination of these two factors that determines the cleaning speed and effectiveness of your pressure washer.

How a Pressure Washer Works

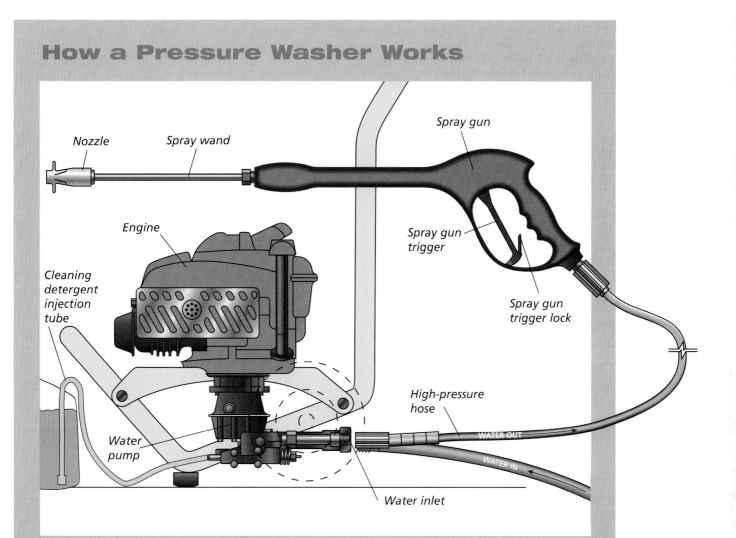

Nozzle   Spray wand

Spray gun

Engine

Spray gun trigger

Cleaning detergent injection tube

Spray gun trigger lock

High-pressure hose

WATER OUT

WATER IN

Water pump

Water inlet

This illustration shows how a basic pressure washer works. Though the principles are the same, actual operation varies from model to model. Consult your owner's manual for specific information regarding your pressure washer.

The supply water travels through the garden hose and enters the **Water Inlet,** filling the **Water Pump.** You must depress the **Spray Gun Trigger** until the **Nozzle** emits a steady stream of water to purge the system of air. A **Bypass Valve** (also called an easy-start valve) allows the water to flow freely through the water pump to prevent pressure from building while you try to start the engine.

When you start the **Engine,** the crankshaft drives a camshaft in the water pump that engages the pistons. The pistons plunge forward to force the water through the pump. When the trigger is not depressed, the pump is in **Bypass Mode** and the water cycles continuously through a series of pump valves. After a few minutes, the circling water heats up; when it reaches 125° to 155°F, a **Thermal Relief Valve** activates and discharges the hot water from the pump, preventing damage to

the system. Fresh, cold water immediately cycles through the pump, deactivating the valve.

Squeezing the spray gun trigger releases the water trapped in the high-pressure hose to activate **Spray Mode.** The **Unloader Valve** redirects the water through the **High-Pressure Outlet,** into the **High-Pressure Hose** and **Spray Wand,** and finally to the nozzle. The nozzle orifice or spray tip contains a small hole that restricts water flow to create pressure as the stream emerges. The shape of this small hole determines the spray pattern.

The **Cleaning Detergent Injection System** activates when the nozzle is set to low-pressure mode. The unrestricted water flow creates a vacuum in the pump that draws the detergent through the **Detergent Injection Tube** and into the water stream.

Releasing the spray gun trigger engages the unloader valve, and the water pump returns to bypass mode. Shutting down the engine stops the entire system. The spray gun trigger lock adds additional safety to prevent accidental spraying.

Water Pressure (PSI) & Water Flow (GPM)

To get the most out of your pressure washer, it is important to consider the application—the more difficult the cleaning project, the more cleaning power your pressure washer must be able to produce. The cleaning power of your pressure washer is based on two factors: water pressure (PSI) and water flow (GPM).

Water pressure is measured in pounds per square inch (PSI). The PSI determines how hard the water spray hits the cleaning surface. This is the force that breaks the bond between dirt and the surface.

Water flow is measured in gallons per minute (GPM) and identifies the amount of water being thrown at a cleaning surface. The GPM dictates the spray's ability to rinse away loosened dirt and grime from the area, and affects the overall cleaning time. A pressure washer with a higher GPM rating cleans faster than a lower-flow unit.

Though most pressure washers are marketed more on PSI, the GPM flow is just as significant to a machine's cleaning ability. A high-flow rate is critical when cleaning horizontal surfaces such as driveways, because the high volume of water will help flush away loosened dirt and grime. However, pressure is more important when cleaning vertical surfaces such as house siding, because gravity helps clear the debris and the additional pressure helps the water travel farther.

In truth, it is the combination of PSI and GPM that determines a pressure washer's cleaning power (or CP). CP offers a better indication of a machine's overall performance, and is useful when comparing pressure washers. To calculate CP, multiply a pressure washer's maximum PSI rating by its GPM flow ($CP = PSI \times GPM$).

For example, a 2500-PSI pressure washer that uses 2.5 GPM generates 6250 CP, while a machine with only 2200 PSI and 3 GPM generates 6600 CP. The results reveal that the second pressure washer has the ability to clean more effectively than the first.

PSI, or "pounds per square inch," *refers to how much force a pressure washer is capable of producing to propel the water stream at the cleaning surface. A pump spray bottle has high water force, but low water flow.*

GPM, or "gallons per minute," *identifies the amount of water a pressure washer uses to clear dirt and grime from the cleaning surface. An unrestricted garden hose illustrates the idea of high water flow and low water force.*

Cleaning Power Affects Cleaning Speed

Ultimately, any size pressure washer can clean any type of surface. However, the CP rating determines how much time it will take to get the job done.

Simply put, pressure washers with higher CP ratings clean faster than lower rated machines. The more Cleaning Power a pressure washer produces, the more surface area it will be able to cover in one pass; the more area it can cover in one pass, the less time it will take to clean the surface. In other words, you can cut your cleaning time significantly by using a pressure washer with a high CP rating.

The diagrams on this page help illustrate how higher rated pressure washers help reduce your overall cleaning time.

**2000 PSI x 2 GPM
4000 CP**

Cleaning Speed: 1X

A pressure washer rated at 4000 CP produces a rather narrow spray pattern, which limits the surface area it can cover in one pass.

**3000 PSI x 3 GPM
9000 CP**

Cleaning Speed: 2X

A pressure washer rated at 9000 CP can cover a much wider area, reducing the number of passes needed to clean the surface.

**4000 PSI x 4 GPM
16000 CP**

Cleaning Speed: 3X

A pressure washer rated at 16000 CP or more is capable of covering much more surface area in fewer passes. Your overall cleaning time will be reduced significantly with a higher rated unit.

Anatomy of a Pressure Washer

These photos show each part of a basic pressure washer. The location of controls and components will vary from model to model. Consult your owner's manual for specific information regarding your pressure washer.

Adjustable Pressure Regulator: Allows operator to control the water pressure output from the water pump. Great feature for reducing cleaning power for delicate surfaces.

Adjustable Spray Nozzle: Nozzle can be adjusted or changed to provide a variety of spray patterns.

Air Filter: Dry type filter element helps keep dirt and dust from entering the engine to prolong engine life.

Automatic Cool Down System: Discharges water out of the pump when it reaches 125° to 155°F to prevent internal pump damage. Also called "Thermal Relief System."

Chassis/Cart: The base and framing of the pressure washer provides easy movement and storage of unit and attachments. Some units contain an Accessory Holder to provide on-board storage for pressure washer attachments and accessories.

Choke Lever: Prepares a cold engine for starting.

Cleaning Detergent Injection Tube: Siphons and filters cleaning detergents or other pressure washer cleaners into the low-pressure water stream.

Engine: Generates the power that runs the pressure washer water pump and system.

Engine Oil Fill: Location for checking and filling engine oil.

Fuel Cap/Tank: Location for filling fuel tank.

High-Pressure Hose: Carries the pressurized water from the water pump to the spray wand.

High-Pressure Outlet: Connection for high-pressure hose.

ProStyle Spray Tips: Interchanging tips provide a variety of spray patterns and more precise cleaning.

Recoil Starter: Provides manual engine-start option.

Spray Gun/Wand: Contains the spray gun, wand extension, and an adjustable nozzle or Quick-Connect spray tips. Uses trigger device with a safety latch to control the application of pressurized water onto a cleaning surface. Nozzles can be adjusted or changed to provide a variety of spray patterns.

Throttle Control Lever: Sets engine in starting mode for recoil starter; stops a running engine. Can be used to adjust the water pressure on some models.

Unloader Valve: Allows water to recirculate within the water pump when the spray gun trigger is not activated.

Water Inlet: Connector for water supply, typically a garden hose.

Water Pump: Pressurizes and directs water to the high-pressure hose. Some units have an adjustable pressure regulator to vary the pressure setting.

Muffler   Choke Lever

Fuel Cap/Tank

On/Off

Throttle Control Lever

Engine

Air Filter

Recoil Starter

High-Pressure Hose

2650 PSI

2.5 GPM
6.5 HP

Spray Gun

ProStyle Spray Tips

Adjustable Spray Nozzle

Adjustable Pressure Regulator

High-Pressure Outlet

Engine Oil Fill

Unloader Valve

Chassis/Cart

Water Pump

Water Inlet

Pressure Washer Engines

Residential-grade pressure washers are powered by one of two sources: electricity or gasoline.

Electric-powered pressure washers are designed for light-duty cleaning, such as washing vehicles and flushing away dirt and debris from patio furniture. Though these units are smaller and less expensive than gas-powered units, the electric motors generally can produce no more than 1750 PSI on a standard 110-volt circuit and have a shorter life expectancy than gas-powered models. Additionally, the power cord limits use to locations where electric power is available and the cord length confines the operating range.

Gas-powered pressure washers provide more power, speed, and freedom than electric-motor units. Residential gas units are rated from 1500 to 4000 PSI, and offer better pressure control, increased durability, and a broader range of accessories. Gas-powered machines are driven by one of two main types of small engines: **Side Valve (L-Head) or Overhead Valve (OHV).**

L-head engines have been the standard for decades, powering lawn mowers and other outdoor equipment. They are small, easy to start, and reliable.

OHV engines are a more recent development, providing more power, better fuel efficiency, and quieter performance over comparable L-head engines. OHV engines also have a longer life expectancy.

Though they differ in design, both engine types operate under the same basic principles and require the same care in order to operate at peak performance. Make sure to observe a consistent engine maintenance schedule, referring to the engine owner's manual for manufacturer's specifications and instructions.

Side Valve (L-head) Engine

Overhead Valve (OHV) Engine

Pressure Washer Water Pumps

In the simplest terms, a pressure washer water pump is the device that forces water through the system at an accelerated rate. While there are many kinds of water pumps, the type used in a pressure washer is known as a positive displacement pump—this means that the amount of water that comes into the device equals the amount of water it pumps out to the high-pressure hose. There are two main types of pressure washer pumps: **Axial Cam** and **Triplex pumps**.

Axial cam pumps, also called wobble plate pumps, are designed for light to medium use by homeowners. These pumps require a water source capable of supplying no less than 20 PSI water pressure and one gallon per minute more than the water-flow capacity of the water pump—the pistons are moved forward by the cam and back by a spring; therefore, do not produce a sufficient vacuum capable of siphoning standing water.

Triplex pumps are the standard for heavy-duty commercial and industrial applications because they have a higher life expectancy and mechanical efficiency than axial cam pumps. They operate in much the same way a car engine works. Triplex pumps positively move the pistons in both directions for more efficient power.

Most pressure washer water pumps are equipped with a Cleaning Detergent Injection System, allowing you to use pressure washer–safe detergents to increase cleaning effectiveness. Setting the nozzle to low-pressure mode creates a vacuum in the pump that draws the detergent through the injection tube and into the water stream. Adjusting the nozzle to high-pressure mode eliminates the vacuum and shuts off the detergent injection system.

Axial Cam Water Pump

Triplex Water Pump

Attachments & Accessories

A pressure washer's engine and water pump produce the power, but it's the attachments and accessories that put that cleaning power in your hands. All models come with a basic package that includes a high-pressure hose, spray wand, and nozzle. Specialty attachments are also available to help enhance cleaning power and provide better nozzle-spray control.

A. **High-Pressure Hoses** carry the pressurized water from the water pump to the spray wand. Most residential pressure washers are equipped with thermo-plastic hose reinforced with nylon, while higher PSI-rated models require hoses made of rubber reinforced with braided steel wire.

B. **The Surface Cleaner** spins 2 nozzles in a circular pattern significantly increasing cleaning speed. The fully enclosed design and soft bristles help contain the spray.

C. **Spray Gun/Wands** control the application of water onto a surface: depressing the spray-gun trigger releases the pressurized water stream in the system; releasing the trigger stops it. A safety latch prevents the trigger from engaging when the spray wand is not in use.

D. **Turbo Nozzles** rotate a 0°-pinpoint jet stream in a wide circular pattern, increasing cleaning effectiveness by up to 40%. This provides an intense water jet for scouring a large surface area faster and more effectively.

E. **Adjustable Nozzles** help control the cleaning power used during pressure washing. Turning the nozzle head adjusts the spray pattern, while sliding it forward and backward changes the pressure between low and high.

F. **Quick-Connect Wand with Spray Tips** provide better spray control and a more consistent spray pattern than adjustable nozzles. Each color-coded spray tip has a designated spray pattern ranging between 0° and 40°, and can be quickly and easily changed via a Quick-Connect fitting on the spray wand.

G. **Brush Attachments** are used to apply cleaning detergents and scrub stubborn stains. Rotating Scrub Brushes, with gear-driven heads and soft bristles, are ideal for vehicles and house siding. Floor Brushes are perfect for large, flat surfaces, such as driveways and garage floors. Utility Brushes (not shown) provide exceptional control on irregular and hard-to-reach surfaces, such as patio furniture and deck railing systems.

H. **Connectors** create air- and watertight seals between hoses and attachments connected to the pressure washer system. There are two standard types of connectors: threaded and Quick-Connect fittings, which allow for quick and simple connections. Retrofit kits are available to convert threaded connectors to Quick-Connect fittings.

I. **Water Broom** speeds up cleaning and provides professional results by providing 3 spray nozzles in a broom like attachment. The base has wheels on it that help you effortlessly move the pressure washer across the surface for consistent cleaning.

J. **The Gutter Cleaner** attaches to your pressure washer wand angling the pressure washer spray down the gutter for more effective cleaning.

Cleaning Detergents & Maintenance Products

Cleaning detergents help break down dirt and grime, making pressure washing easier and more effective. Use only detergents manufactured for pressure washer use; unapproved cleaners may not be environmentally friendly and may damage the water pump and other attachments.

Pressure washer cleaning detergents are typically sold in one-gallon containers of pre-mixed or concentrated formulas. There are a variety of detergents available, each specially formulated for specific applications.

A. **Multi-Purpose/Vehicle Wash** cuts through saturated dirt and grime on a variety of surfaces, including driveways, vehicles and boats.

B. **Deck & Siding Wash** cleans and brightens wooden decks, siding and fences.

C. **Heavy-Duty Degreaser** helps remove grease, oil, and other stains from concrete surfaces.

D. **Mold & Mildew Remover** kills mold and mildew growth on siding, concrete, brick and other surfaces.

E. **O-Ring Maintenance Kit** contains replacement O-rings, rubber washers, screen filters, and a wire tool for cleaning nozzles.

F. **Pump Oil** keeps water pump parts lubricated to prevent pump seizure.

G. **Fresh Start®** stabilizes gas left in engine tanks over long storage periods to help prevent carburetor damage.

H. **PumpSaver™** prevents damage during winter storage with a unique antifreeze and lubricant formula to protect seals and pistons.

I. **Startup/Store Kit** is used to condition parts before or after long storage periods.

J. **Briggs & Stratton's Small Engine Care & Repair** is the essential guide to maintaining your pressure washer engine.

Basic
OPERATION
& TECHNIQUES

BASIC OPERATION & TECHNIQUES

Operating a pressure washer can be easy and fun: connect a water supply, start the engine, and pull the spray-gun trigger to blast away years of unsightly dirt and grime from your deck, siding, and driveway. The only real technique to learn is how to control the cleaning power from the nozzle spray.

Although different surfaces require different spray patterns and pressure settings, it is not difficult to determine the appropriate cleaning approach for each project. The nozzle is adjustable, providing a range of possibilities—from a low-pressure, wide-fan spray for general cleaning and rinsing to a narrow, intense stream for stubborn stains and paint stripping.

Some pressure washers include an adjustable pressure regulator on the engine or water pump that allows you to regulate the pressure at the machine itself. But the quickest and easiest adjustment you can make is to change the distance between the nozzle and the surface being cleaned—simply move closer to the surface for more intense cleaning power and move back from the surface for less intense cleaning.

As you begin using your pressure washer, you will quickly learn the basic cleaning techniques to achieve the best results. And over time, you will develop your own techniques and tricks for faster, more effective pressure washing.

Safety & Precautions

Although pressure washing is easier and more efficient than traditional cleaning methods, observing a few simple precautions will ensure your cleaning project is completed successfully and safely.

Operational Safety

✔ Read both the owner's manual and engine manual in their entirety before operating your pressure washer.
✔ Make sure the unit is on a stable surface and the cleaning area has adequate slopes and drainage to prevent puddles.
✔ Do not run the power washer before connecting and turning on the water supply—failing to do so will result in damage to the pump.
✔ Always keep the high-pressure hose connected to both the pump and the spray gun while the system is pressurized.
✔ Never refuel a hot or running engine. Wait two minutes before refueling.

Usage Safety

✔ Assume a solid stance, and firmly grasp the spray gun with both hands to avoid injury if the gun kicks back.
✔ Use extreme caution when spraying near power lines, service feeds, and electrical meters.
✔ Keep the nozzle spray away from electrical wiring and windows.
✔ Do not secure the spray gun in the open position.
✔ Never adjust the spray pattern or change a spray tip while spraying.
✔ Using a pressure washer from a ladder, scaffolding, or other unstable position is not recommended. A slip or fall could result from the recoil of the initial spray, or the pressure of the water striking a wall surface.

Personal Safety

✔ Never aim the nozzle at people or animals—the high-pressure stream of water can pierce skin and its underlying tissues, resulting in serious injury.
✔ Never allow children to operate the pressure washer. Do not leave a pressure washer unattended while it is running.
✔ Do not wear open-toed shoes while pressure washing.
✔ Most importantly, always wear eye protection when using a pressure washer or when in the vicinity of the equipment in use—the high-pressure spray can cause paint chips or other particles to become airborne.
✔ Always squeeze the gun trigger after use to relieve the pressure in the gun, hose and pump.

Operating Your Pressure Washer

Before starting your pressure washer, you must prepare the unit for use. Make sure to check the engine oil level each time you use your pressure washer—any attempt to crank or start the engine before it has been properly serviced could result in equipment failure or damage. If your pressure washer is new, check the oil often during engine break-in.

When changing or adding oil, do not overfill the engine crankcase. Overfilling oil may cause smoking, hard starting, spark plug fouling, and oil saturation of the air filter. Refer to both the pressure washer and engine owner's manuals for oil recommendations and filling instructions for your particular make and model.

As you hook up your pressure washer, it is a good idea to check all hoses, screens, O-rings, and attachments for wear or damage to help avoid any problems during operation. See "Preventative Maintenance" on page 99.

Finally, make sure the fuel tank is filled to the proper level prior to starting the engine. Fill the tank with clean, fresh, lead-free regular gasoline, but do not overfill; allow space for fuel expansion. If the engine has been running, turn off the pressure washer and let it cool for at least two minutes before removing the gas cap.

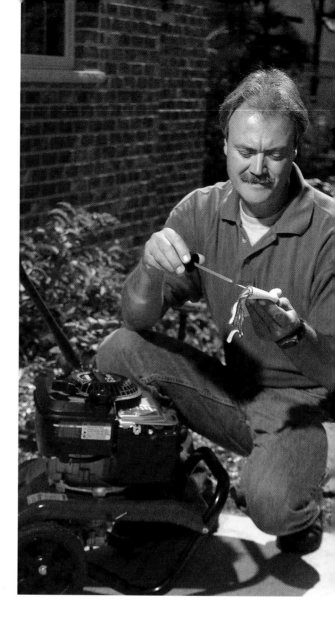

Preparing the Work Site

Before starting any pressure washing project, it is important to take the time to properly prepare the work site:

✔ Cover any nearby electrical equipment, such as meters and air conditioning units, and any outdoor lighting fixtures.
✔ Water and cover any plants or shrubbery that may come in contact with cleaning detergents or the nozzle spray. (Pressure washers have enough power to shred plants.)
✔ Remove any obstructions from the area, such as vehicles, outdoor furniture, and yard decorations.
✔ Close all nearby windows and doors.
✔ Sweep away any large debris from horizontal surfaces.

Connecting High-Pressure Hoses & Water Supply

A pressure washer typically requires an outside water source capable of supplying cold water (less than 100°F) at no less than 20 PSI and a flow rate 1 GPM greater than the units rating. (Higher-rated pressure washers may require a greater water supply flow rate.) Most homes' outdoor faucets supply 40 PSI of water pressure and have flow rates around 8 GPM.

To connect the water supply to the pressure washer pump, use a standard garden hose no longer than 50 feet in length. There must be at least 10 feet of unrestricted garden hose between the pump inlet and any flow shut-off device, such as a 'Y' shut-off connector or other water shut-off valve.

Use a high-pressure hose no longer than 100 feet—longer hoses can cause a decrease in water pressure and problems with the detergent injection system. If the hose has kinks, cuts, or other damage, replace it immediately with a new high-pressure hose—designed for pressure washer use—that exceeds the maximum pressure rating of your pressure washer. Never replace a high-pressure hose with a hose designated for another purpose.

1 *Attach the wand extension to the spray gun; make sure the connection is tight.*

2 *Attach one end of the high-pressure hose to the base of the spray gun. For Quick-Connect fittings, gently tug on the hose to make sure the connection is tight.*

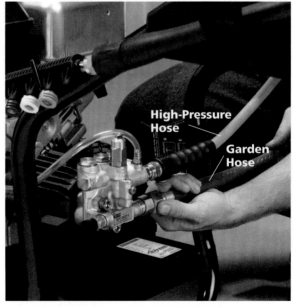

High-Pressure Hose

Garden Hose

3 *Attach the other end of the high-pressure hose to the pump's high-pressure outlet. Run water through the garden hose until the hose is cleaned out of any debris, then connect it to the pump's water inlet.*

Starting Your Pressure Washer

With the oil and fuel at recommended levels and all the hoses connected, your pressure washer is ready to be started. Make sure to operate your pressure washer outdoors only. Even an open garage is not safe. Take a moment to review the unit's assembly to ensure all connections are tight and that the nozzle is in low-pressure mode (see below). To start the engine, follow the instructions in the engine owner's manual.

When starting the engine, keep the safety latch on the spray wand locked to prevent the trigger from accidentally engaging. If the recoil starter is hard to pull or the engine fails to start, squeeze the spray-gun trigger to relieve internal pump pressure.

Always wear eye protection when using your pressure washer.

If the pressure washer is not equipped with an easy start feature, squeeze the spray-gun trigger to relieve the pressure in the water pump. Hold the trigger until there is a steady stream of water, then engage the safety latch and attempt to start the engine again.

Using Spray Nozzles

Pressure washer spray wands come equipped with one of two nozzle designs: adjustable nozzles or Quick-Connect spray tips. Both options provide a wide range of spray patterns and pressure settings, but Quick-Connect spray tips produce a more consistent spray pattern than adjustable nozzles because each tip is a set to a specific spray pattern.

When adjusting the nozzle or changing tips, always engage the trigger safety latch and never put your hands in front of the nozzle. As a general rule, use the wide-angle spray patterns for general cleaning and rinsing, and the narrow-angle patterns for scouring stains, reaching high surfaces (such as the second story of a house), and stripping paint.

Note: The 0°-pinpoint spray pattern produces an intense water jet capable of causing damage to delicate surfaces, such as wood. Use caution when using this spray pattern.

USING AN ADJUSTABLE NOZZLE

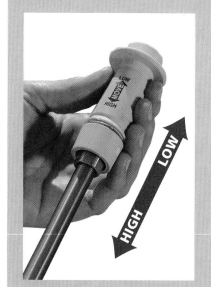

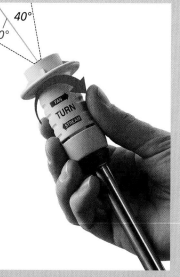

1 To change the pressure setting, slide the nozzle head forward to activate low-pressure mode for applying cleaning detergents. Move the nozzle head backward to activate high-pressure mode for cleaning and rinsing surfaces.

2 Twist the nozzle head left or right to adjust the spray pattern, from a 0°-pinpoint stream to a 40°-wide fan spray.

BASIC OPERATION

Using Quick-Connect Spray Tips

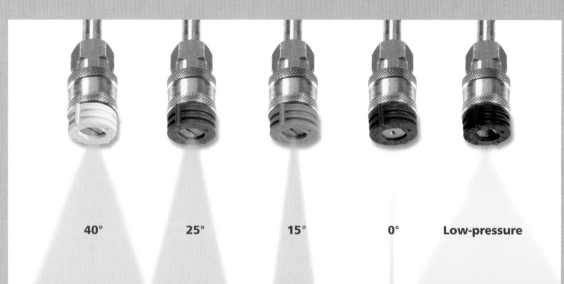

| 40° | 25° | 15° | 0° | Low-pressure |

Quick-Connect spray tips have fixed spray patterns that are more consistent than those produced by an adjustable nozzle. Each tip is color-coded for easy identification. **White (40°):** produces a wide-fan spray for general cleaning and rinsing. **Green (25°):** provides a narrower-fan spray for tough stains in general cleaning applications. **Yellow (15°):** maintains a tight-fan spray with intense cleaning power for heavy-duty cleaning and paint preparation. **Red (0°):** creates a concentrated pinpoint water jet for stubborn stains on concrete, masonry, or steel, and for stripping paint. **Black (low-pressure):** emits a low-pressure water stream for applying cleaning detergents. The detergent injection system will engage only with this tip in place.

1 Engage the trigger safety latch on the spray wand. Pull back the Quick-Connect collar on the wand extension, and remove the current spray tip.

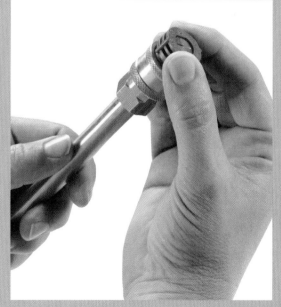

2 Select the desired spray tip, insert it into the fitting, and release the collar. Tug on spray tip to make sure the connection is secure. Rotate to desired spray angle.

Adjusting the Cleaning Power

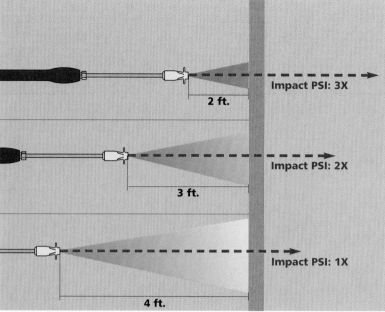

Method 1. Adjust the Distance: *The fastest and easiest way to control the pressure is to change the distance between the nozzle and the cleaning surface—move the nozzle back from the surface to reduce the PSI at the point of impact; move the nozzle closer to intensify it.*

The key to fast, effective, and, successful pressure washing is control of the Cleaning Power at the surface. This is achieved by adjusting the pressure washer to accommodate the demands of the cleaning surface—dirtier surfaces will need more Cleaning Power while less dirty surfaces require a lower setting.

Cleaning Power can be altered in three ways: Method 1. adjust the distance between the nozzle and the cleaning surface; Method 2. change the nozzle spray pattern; or Method 3. adjust the water pressure output at the engine or water pump. Each of these methods will create the desired effects, though often a combination of adjustments will provide the best results.

Refer to "Water Pressure & Water Flow" on pages 14 and 15 for more information regarding cleaning power and cleaning time.

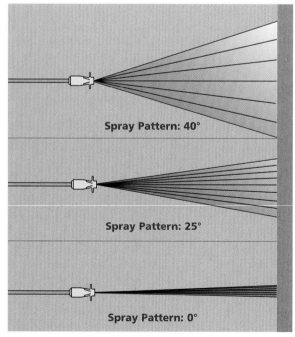

Method 2. Change the Spray Pattern: *As the spray pattern widens, the impact of the water pressure and cleaning power at the surface is reduced. If you need to maintain higher pressure at a distance, such as to clean the second story of a house, consider a narrower spray pattern.*

Method 3. Adjust the Water Pressure Output at the Engine or Water Pump: *Some models have an adjustable pressure regulator knob on the engine or water pump that allows you to adjust the water pressure output. This enables you to fine-tune the water pressure without altering the distance or spray pattern.*

Testing the Cleaning Power

Prior to starting your pressure washing project, it is best to test the cleaning power on the actual surface to be cleaned. This simple step will help determine the most appropriate and effective equipment settings to avoid mistakes and ensure the best results.

Choose an inconspicuous area of the cleaning surface for the test, such as a corner of a deck or a back wall of a garage. Start with a wide-fan spray and hold the nozzle at least four to five feet from the surface, moving closer as needed. When examining the test area, look for signs of damage or potential problems before making any adjustments.

The effective cleaning power will vary from project to project. Durable materials, such as concrete and masonry, can withstand higher Impact PSI levels and may actually require an intensified pressure setting. However, softer, more delicate surfaces, especially wood and painted surfaces, can be damaged under a high Impact PSI. The best approach is to reduce the cleaning power and use a pressure washer cleaning detergent, taking multiple passes over heavily soiled areas.

Note: The 0°-pinpoint spray pattern produces an intense water jet capable of causing damage to delicate surfaces, especially wood. Use caution when using this spray pattern.

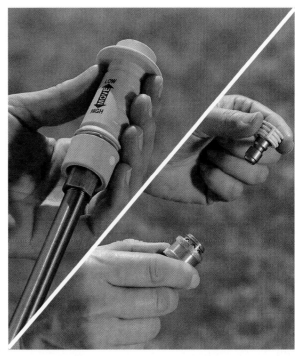

1 *Engage the trigger safety latch, then slide the adjustable nozzle backward to high-pressure mode and twist to a wide-fan spray, or install the white (40°) Quick-Connect spray tip.*

2 *Firmly grasp the spray wand with both hands. Hold the nozzle approximately four to five feet from an inconspicuous area of the cleaning surface. Release the trigger safety latch and apply the high-pressure spray to the test area.*

3 *Check the test area—the spray should remove dirt and stains without causing damage to the surface. Make any necessary adjustments to the cleaning power (opposite page). Once you determine the appropriate Impact PSI, continue pressure washing.*

Basic Cleaning Techniques

Pressure washing is quite simple: firmly grasp the spray wand with both hands, depress the trigger and move the nozzle spray across the surface to be cleaned. However, understanding a few basic techniques will help you work faster, safer, and more efficiently. To successfully pressure wash any surface, remember these five basic tips:

✓ When cleaning a new surface, start with a wide spray pattern and hold the nozzle four to five feet from the surface. Move closer to the surface until the desired effect is achieved.

✓ Keep the nozzle in motion, spraying at a steady speed with long, even strokes to ensure consistent results.

✓ Maintain a consistent distance between the nozzle and the cleaning surface.

✓ When cleaning heavily soiled or stained surfaces, use cleaning detergents formulated for pressure washers (pages 34 to 35).

✓ Consider using brush attachments or a turbo nozzle to help remove stubborn dirt, grime, and stains (page 37).

In addition, the following techniques will help you clean faster and more effectively with your pressure washer.

Always keep the nozzle in motion, spraying at a steady speed and using long, even strokes. Take multiple passes over heavily soiled areas. Take care not to dwell on one spot for too long, especially when using narrow, high-pressure spray patterns.

Hold the spray wand so that the nozzle distributes the spray pattern across the surface evenly. Holding the nozzle at too low an angle can cause an uneven spray pattern, resulting in "zebra striping." Also, maintain a consistent distance between the nozzle and the cleaning surface to ensure consistent results and help flush dirt and debris from the area.

Work in identifiable sections, such as the area between the expansion joints in concrete. If there is a slope, work downhill to promote drainage and help flush away dirt and debris. Wet entire surface to prevent streaking.

When pressure washing lap siding or wood, keep the spray pattern within the width of one to two boards.

To prevent streaks on vertical surfaces, such as fencing and house siding, always begin pressure washing or applying cleaning detergent (see pages 34 to 35) at the bottom of the surface, then work upward.

When rinsing vertical surfaces, start at the top and work downward. Gravity will help the clean water flush away dirt, debris, and detergent residue, in addition to preventing streaks.

To clean out-of-reach surfaces, such as the second story of a house, use a narrow spray pattern to propel the water stream up to the surface. While enough cleaning power will remain to be effective, the spray pattern will be somewhat inconsistent and may require multiple passes. Stand behind and to the side of the spray to avoid getting wet and make sure to widen the spray pattern as you work downward.

Using Cleaning Detergents

Pressure washing alone is enough to clean most surfaces, but for stubborn stains or mold and mildew, the use of cleaning detergents can help make cleaning easier and more effective.

Most pressure washers are equipped with a detergent injection system. The nozzle must be in low-pressure mode to apply detergents. This helps the detergent cling to the surface and remain there long enough to be effective. Most detergents require a dwell time of 5 to 10 minutes before being rinsed.

There are a wide variety of liquid detergents specifically designed for particular pressure washer applications. Though most detergents are biodegradable, always flush the surrounding area with plenty of clear water. Never use bleach or bleach-based products, which may cause damage to the water pump and kill vegetation. Only use cleaning detergents that are safe for pressure washer use and always follow the manufacturer's instructions on the container.

1 *Choose a cleaning detergent appropriate to the application (see page 21). Detergents are typically sold in one-gallon containers, pre-mixed or concentrated. Prepare the detergent, following the manufacturer's instructions on the container.*

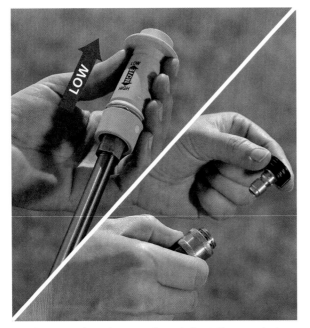

2 *Engage the trigger safety. Adjust the nozzle to low-pressure mode, or install the black spray tip.*

3 *Insert the injection tube and filter into the cleaning detergent, or fill the detergent reservoir.*

4 *Disengage the trigger safety. Depress the trigger until the detergent is present in the water stream, and then apply detergent to an identifiable section of the cleaning surface. On vertical surfaces, work from bottom to top to avoid streaks.*

5 *Allow the detergent to dwell on the surface for the allotted time, as specified by the manufacturer, typically 5 to 10 minutes. Do not let the detergent dry; re-spray if necessary.*

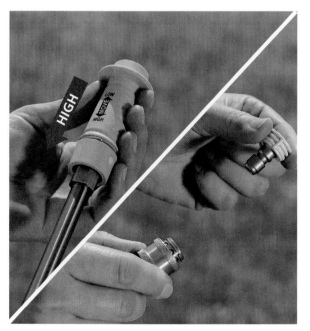

6 *Engage the trigger safety. Adjust the nozzle to high-pressure mode, or install the desired spray tip. Depress the trigger to clear the remaining detergent from the system.*

7 *Test the cleaning power (page 31) and adjust as needed. Thoroughly rinse off detergent residue. On vertical surfaces, work from top to bottom to avoid streaks. When finished, flush the surrounding area with plenty of clear water to disperse the detergent to prevent harm to vegetation.*

Shutting Down Your Pressure Washer

With your pressure washing project complete, follow the instructions in the owner's manual for shutting down the unit. Let the engine idle for two minutes before shutdown, and let it cool off before you store it.

Also, make sure to turn off the water supply and relieve the trapped in-line pressure in the system before disconnecting hoses. Clean all attachments and accessories with clear water and drain any remaining liquids from the hoses prior to storage.

If the pressure washer will be stored for more than 30 days after use, allow the engine to cool, then disconnect the spark-plug lead from the spark plug and pull the recoil handle five to six times to remove any liquid from the water pump. Inject pump saver and store your pressure washer and accessories in a clean, dry place.

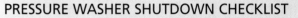

Pat Simpson:
PRO TIP

PRESSURE WASHER SHUTDOWN CHECKLIST

When shutting down your pressure washer, remember to:

- Flush the cleaning detergent injection system.
- Let the engine idle for two minutes prior to shutdown.
- Turn off the water supply and relieve the pressure in the system.
- Disconnect all hoses and attachments.
- Empty pump of remaining liquids.
- Inject pump saver into pump.
- Store your pressure washer and attachments in a cool, dry place.

Clean the detergent injection system after each use to prevent clogging or damage: Place the injection tube and filter in a bucket of clear, clean water. Adjust the nozzle to low-pressure mode, or install the black spray tip. Depress the spray trigger and flush the system for one to two minutes.

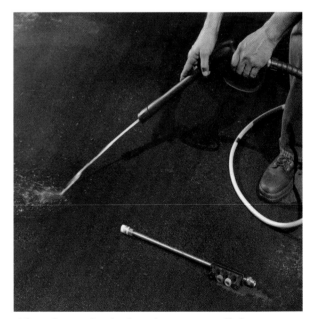

After the engine is shut down, turn off the water supply, and then always squeeze the spray trigger to relieve the trapped in-line pressure in the system. Disconnect the hoses from the water pump, and then empty the pump of all remaining liquids by pulling the recoil handle six times—a small amount of water will come out of the pump's water outlet.

Using Pressure Washer Accessories

There are a number of specialty accessories available for your pressure washer, each designed to help save time and increase cleaning effectiveness. They attach directly to the spray gun in place of the wand extension. Be sure to follow the manufacturer's instructions when using any specialty attachment.

The most widely available accessories are brush attachments and the turbo nozzle. Brush attachments operate in low-pressure mode, allowing you to scrub heavily soiled areas while applying cleaning detergents to penetrate set stains and grime. There are three main styles of brush attachments: rotating scrub brushes have gear-driven heads with soft bristles, ideal for vehicles, fences, and house siding; floor brushes look like shop push brooms and are perfect for heavy stains and impacted dirt on driveways and other flat surfaces; and utility brushes provide exceptional control on irregular or hard-to-reach surfaces, such as deck railings systems and patio furniture.

Turbo nozzles or rotary nozzles spin a 0°-jet stream in a circular pattern, providing an intense wide-spray pattern for scouring large surface areas faster and more effectively. A turbo nozzle can easily cut through heavy oil and grease stains on concrete, brick, and plastic and strip paint from various surfaces; however, do not use this accessory on delicate materials, especially wood.

Use brush attachments to scrub impacted dirt and heavily soiled areas on a variety of surfaces. Applying cleaning detergents with a scrub brush allows the product to penetrate heavy grime and stains to better dissolve the bond between dirt and the surface. The brush bristles also help to clear wastewater and debris from the cleaning area.

When using a turbo nozzle, always start at a great distance from the surface, much farther than when using a standard nozzle spray. Move closer as needed to achieve the desired effect. Always keep the turbo nozzle in constant motion; never dwell on a single spot. Pass over stubborn stains repeatedly until they are gone, using even strokes. Never use a turbo nozzle on wood surfaces—the powerful jet stream could damage wood fibers.

Pat Simpson:
PRO TIP

THE TURBO NOZZLE ADVANTAGE

Perhaps the single most effective accessory you can purchase for your pressure washer is the turbo nozzle. This accessory rotates a 0°-jet stream in a circular pattern 5,000 to 9,000 RPMs, increasing effective cleaning power by up to 50%. It is a huge time saver and can more effectively remove stubborn stains.

CLEANING PROJECTS

CLEANING PROJECTS

Whether washing mold and mildew from your house, removing oil and grease deposits from your driveway, or stripping old finish from your deck, a pressure washer accomplishes the project in a fraction of the time it takes using traditional methods. To successfully pressure wash any surface, remember these five basic tips:

✓ Keep the nozzle in motion, spraying at a steady speed with long, even strokes to ensure uniform results.
✓ Maintain a consistent distance between the nozzle and the cleaning surface.
✓ To prevent streaks on vertical surfaces, apply cleaning detergents from bottom to top and rinse from top to bottom.
✓ When cleaning heavily soiled or stained surfaces, use cleaning detergents formulated for pressure washers.
✓ Consider using brush attachments and a turbo nozzle to help remove stubborn dirt, grime, and stains.

Before beginning any cleaning project, make sure to properly prepare the work site to ensure safe and efficient pressure washing. In addition, always test the nozzle spray on an inconspicuous area of the cleaning surface to determine the most effective cleaning power. Remember that the easiest way to adjust the cleaning power is to simply change the distance between the nozzle and the cleaning surface: move away from the surface to reduce Impact PSI or move closer to intensify it.

For other basic pressure washer operations and cleaning techniques, see pages 22 to 37.

Portfolio of Uses: Before & After

BEFORE

CLEANING A TRUCK

A pressure washer takes the work out of cleaning a dirty truck. The high-pressure spray can cut through thick dirt and grime, clear mud-impacted joints and wheel wells, and penetrate ground-in stains on a textured bed liner. Using a Vehicle & Boat Wash cleaning detergent with a rotating scrub brush can help restore a dull paint finish to a like-new appearance.

AFTER

RESTORING A WEATHERED DECK

With a pressure washer, you can clean a deck in a fraction of the time it would take using traditional methods. A quick rinse can remove superficial dirt and grime, while a thorough wash can strip layers of old sealer-preservative to prepare the surface for refinishing. In addition, the various spray pattern settings make cleaning the railing system nearly effortless.

BEFORE

AFTER

CLEANING BRICK WALKWAYS & PATIOS

A blast from a pressure washer can restore brick walkways and patios to their original vibrant color. If mold and mildew is a problem, simply treat it with a Mold & Mildew Remover detergent to kill the existing growth and deter its regrowth. Scrub brush attachments can also be used to remove water stains, rust, and efflorescence to help return your brickwork to its former beauty.

BEFORE

AFTER

CLEANING EAVES & OVERHANGS

The eaves, soffits, and overhangs of your house can be quickly cleaned with a pressure washer. Adjusting the nozzle to a tight spray pattern allows you to propel the water stream upward to reach high surfaces and hard-to-reach areas. Multi-Purpose and House Wash detergents will help cut built-up dirt and grime for faster, more efficient cleaning.

BEFORE

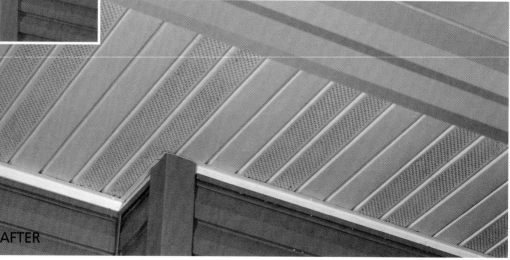

AFTER

CLEANING PROJECTS

CLEANING AN RV

Washing a recreational vehicle (RV) can be a labor-intensive chore, but with the aid of a pressure washer, your workload will be reduced dramatically. A wide spray pattern can scour mud and grime along the bottom of the vehicle, while a tighter water stream can reach dust and dirt along the top. You'll be ready for the open road in no time.

BEFORE

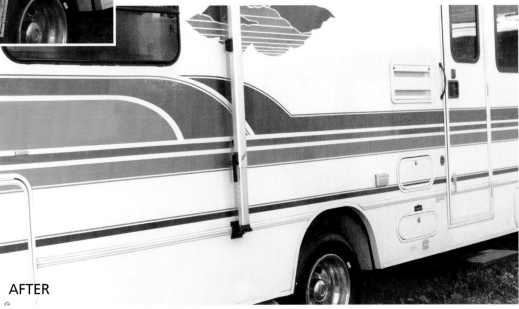

AFTER

STRIPPING PAINT

Preparing a house or other surface for a fresh coat of paint is another time-consuming project that a pressure washer can simplify. The powerful jet stream can strip old, peeling paint easily and efficiently, without the need for a ladder or hand scraper. You'll be able to sand, prime, and paint in a matter of hours rather than days.

AFTER   BEFORE

BEFORE

CLEANING A LAWN MOWER

A lawn mower is a magnet for grass, leaves, and dirt that can, over time, hinder performance and damage engine parts. A quick cleaning with a pressure washer can remove heavy grime and debris around the mower blade and chassis to help prevent costly repairs. Never get engines wet as this may cause damage.

AFTER

BEFORE

CLEANING CONCRETE GARAGE FLOORS

Oil, grease, paint, and fertilizer stains can be removed from a concrete garage floor with a pressure washer. Heavy-Duty Degreaser detergents help break down the bond between stains and concrete, while a turbo nozzle effectively cuts through deposits and flushes away debris to make your garage floor look like a freshly poured slab.

AFTER

CLEANING PROJECTS

AFTER

BEFORE

RESTORING A WOOD FENCE

Give new life to a weathered wood fence through the use of your pressure washer. A quick rinse can remove surface dirt and grime, while a thorough wash with a pressure washer formulated detergent can eliminate stains including sap, oil, moss and mildew. The high-pressure spray can also strip old paint and sealers to help restore your fence to its original beauty, like the day it was installed.

CLEANING A VINYL FENCE

Pressure washing is the fastest and easiest method of cleaning a vinyl fence. Often a quick rinse with a high-pressure spray is enough to remove dust and dirt, while adding a Multi-Purpose Wash detergent can cut through tough grime and stubborn stains, restoring the vinyl's original, glossy finish.

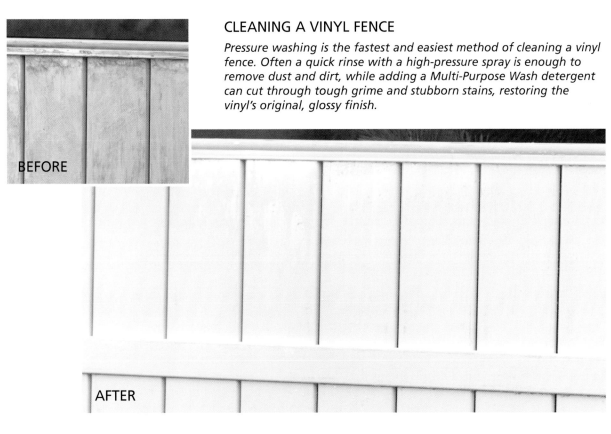

BEFORE

AFTER

Housing Exteriors

Over time, sun, pollution, and weather all contribute to the deterioration of housing exteriors. Some surfaces simply fade, while others turn chalky and porous. All housing exteriors are also susceptible to dirt and mildew buildup, which is not only unsightly, but can also be hiding damaged surfaces.

Pressure washing is the most effective and efficient method of cleaning housing exteriors. The high-pressure water stream can penetrate the textured surface of aluminum, vinyl, and wood sidings, as well as stucco and brick. Removing surface dirt and grime often requires only a quick rinse of cold water. More substantial stains or mildew buildup need to be treated with a cleaning detergent.

Cleaning an average-sized house takes about 3 to 6 hours, depending on the cleaning requirements and size of the building. Spraying off dust and dirt before winter arrives each year will also keep the house looking better, longer. Pressure washing is also ideal for awnings, soffits, fascia, window trim, and foundation walls.

Identifying the Problem

(left) **General dust and dirt on siding** can be removed easily using a high-pressure rinse with a wide spray pattern. On heavily soiled areas, use House Wash or Multi-Purpose cleaning detergent and a Rotating Scrub Brush to help penetrate and scour stains.

(above) **Mold is identifiable by its blackish appearance** and strong bond to house siding. For best results when treating mold, apply a Mold & Mildew Remover cleaning detergent to loosen the bond and use a Rotating Scrub Brush or Utility Brush attachment to scrub heavily soiled areas.

Mildew has a greenish appearance and is easily treated with a Mold & Mildew Remover cleaning detergent. Apply Mold & Mildew Remover with a Rotating Scrub Brush to clean faster and more effectively.

Aluminum siding can turn chalky white after many years of exposure to sun and pollution. Often a high-pressure rinse with a wide spray pattern and mild cleaning power is enough to clean the surface. In more severe cases, apply a House Wash or Multi-Purpose cleaning detergent and increase the cleaning power during the final rinse.

Cleaning Siding

Whether cleaning aluminum, vinyl, or wood siding, you will save time and work more efficiently using a pressure washer.

Pressure washing is a surefire method for revitalizing chalky, dingy aluminum siding and preparing it for a fresh coat of paint. To prevent stripping paint or denting aluminum siding, use a wide spray pattern.

When vinyl begins to look dull or soiled, pressure washing will quickly restore its original color and finish.

As with wooden decks and fences (see pages 58 to 65), pressure washing wood siding can remove gray, deteriorated fibers and strip old sealer-preservatives and paint, exposing the natural beauty hidden beneath years of weather damage and neglect. After wood siding is cleaned, seal it with a fresh coat of sealer-preservative or paint to maintain its integrity and appearance.

As you work, take care not to spray under lap siding—water trapped behind siding can damage sheathing and insulation, and can weep out, causing streaks and stains. Additionally, do not aim the spray at windows or other fragile materials.

PRESTART CHECKLIST:

Tools & Materials:

✓ Pressure Washer
✓ 50 to 100 feet of High-Pressure Hose
✓ Cleaning Detergent Formulated for Pressure Washers

✓ Eye Protection

Optional
✓ Rotating Scrub Brush

Site Preparation:

1. Remove any obstacles from the work area.
2. Wet and cover nearby plants and vegetation.
3. Cover nearby electrical components, including light fixtures.
4. Close all nearby windows and doors.

CLEANING PERFORMANCE:

Recommended Spray Pattern:

40° Spray Pattern or White Spray Tip

Recommended Distance:

PSI Rating:	Nozzle Distance:
2000 or less	10 in. to 24 in.
2000 to 3000	12 in. to 24 in.
3000 or more	18 in. to 36 in.

1 *Adjust the nozzle to low-pressure mode: slide the adjustable nozzle forward or install the black spray tip. Prepare the cleaning detergent according to the manufacturer's instructions, and insert the detergent injection tube and filter into the container.*

2 *Depress the spray trigger until detergent is present in the water stream, then apply to the surface, working from bottom to top in identifiable sections. Allow detergent to dwell for 5 to 10 minutes. Do not let detergent dry; rewet as needed.*

VARIATION: *Use a Rotating Scrub Brush attachment to help penetrate heavily soiled areas and scour built-up grime.*

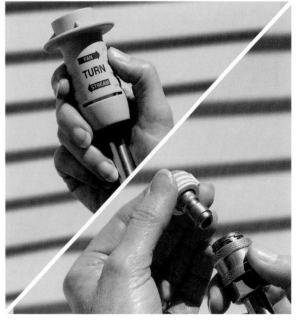

3 *Adjust the nozzle to high-pressure mode: slide the adjustable nozzle backward and twist to a wide spray pattern, or install the white 40°-spray tip. Depress the spray trigger to flush any remaining detergent from the line.*

Cleaning Siding (continued)

4 *Test the cleaning power on an inconspicuous area of the surface and make any necessary adjustments (pages 30 to 31). Rinse off detergent residue, working from top to bottom and covering one to two laps with the spray pattern. Move on to the next section to continue cleaning.*

Second Story Cleaning

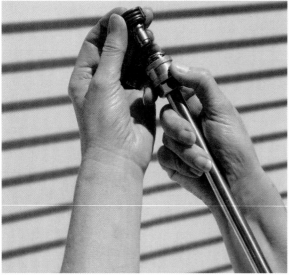

1 *To clean second-story sections or walls taller than 12 feet: twist the adjustable nozzle to a narrower spray pattern or install the yellow 15° or red 0°-spray tip to propel the water stream to out-of-reach areas.*

2 *As you work downward, be sure to increase your distance from the house surface. Lower the cleaning power and widen the spray pattern as you move down the wall section.*

Cleaning Soffits & Gutters

1 When pressure washing soffits and gutters, first rinse the soffits to help prevent streaks or spots caused by dripping wastewater and detergent residue from the gutters.

2 Work along the length of the overhang, standing back and to the side of the nozzle spray to help keep deflected water from hitting you.

Restoring Wood Siding

When pressure washing wood, observe the same precautions as for restoring wood decks and fences (see pages 58 to 65). The most common mistake is using too much cleaning power, which can cause wood fibers to fray, causing the surface to appear fuzzy. To repair such damage, scrub the affected area with a soft-bristle brush or sand with a fine-grit paper. Do not use steel wool or any type of metal on wood. After pressure washing wood siding, seal with a fresh coat of sealer-preservative or paint. Note: To strip wood siding in preparation for repainting, see "Stripping Paint" on pages 80 to 83.

Cleaning Stucco

Over time, the textured surface of stucco walls will collect substantial dust and dirt. A quick high-pressure rinse with cold water is often enough to flush away such unsightly buildup. For heavier stains, a complete wash with a cleaning detergent may be required.

When pressure washing stucco, always use a wide spray pattern and hold the nozzle at a 45° angle at least 24 inches from the surface to prevent damage to the finish. To kill mildew and algae, treat the area with a high-pressure rinse of clear water, then apply a Mold & Mildew Remover, followed by a second high-pressure rinse.

Rust and copper stains from leaky outdoor faucets are another common problem with stucco. Home centers and hardware stores carry a number of copper and ferrous stain removers that will effectively take care of the job. After treatment, thoroughly pressure wash the area with plenty of clear water.

PRESTART CHECKLIST:

Tools:
- ✓ Pressure Washer
- ✓ 50 to 100 feet of High-Pressure Hose
- ✓ Cleaning Detergent Formulated for Pressure Washers
- ✓ Eye Protection

Optional
- ✓ Rotating Scrub Brush
- ✓ Rust Remover
- ✓ Soft-Bristle Brush

Site Prep:
1. Remove any obstacles from the work area.
2. Wet and cover nearby plants and vegetation.
3. Cover nearby electrical components.
4. Close all nearby windows and doors.

CLEANING PERFORMANCE:

Recommended Spray Pattern:

40° Spray Pattern or White Spray Tip

Recommended Distance:

PSI Rating:	Nozzle Distance:
2000 or less	12 in. to 24 in.
2000 to 3000	18 in. to 30 in.
3000 or more	42 in. to 60 in.

1 *Prior to pressure washing, patch any cracks or chips in the stucco surface to prevent water from seeping behind walls. Allow patched areas to dry for at least one week before pressure washing.*

2 *Adjust the nozzle to low-pressure mode: slide the adjustable nozzle forward or install the black spray tip. Prepare the cleaning detergent according to the manufacturer's instructions, and insert the detergent injection tube and filter into the container.*

3 *Depress the spray trigger until detergent is present in the water stream, then apply to the surface, working from bottom to top in sections. Allow detergent to dwell for 5 to 10 minutes. Do not let detergent dry; rewet as needed.*

VARIATION: *Use a Rotating Scrub Brush attachment to help penetrate heavily soiled areas and scour built-up grime.*

Cleaning Stucco (continued)

4 *Adjust the nozzle to high-pressure mode: slide the adjustable nozzle backward and twist to a wide spray pattern, or install the white 40°-spray tip. Depress the spray trigger to flush any remaining detergent from the line.*

5 *Test the cleaning power on an inconspicuous area of the surface and make any necessary adjustments (pages 30 to 31). Rinse off detergent residue, working in identifiable sections, from top to bottom. Move on to the next section to continue cleaning.*

6 *Lightly scrub stubborn rust and copper stains using a soft-bristle brush and a Rust Remover product; follow the manufacturer's instructions.*

7 *After treating rust and copper stains, rinse the area with plenty of clear water, using a wide spray pattern.*

Cleaning Brick & Mortar

Pressure washing can restore weather-beaten brick and mortar to its former glory. There are a wide variety of brick types, and though they all appear to be quite durable, most are actually rather soft. The best approach when pressure washing brick is less Impact PSI and more cleaning detergent.

However, dry brick absorbs liquids, including detergents, which can cause discoloration. Make sure to thoroughly pre-soak the brick before applying the detergent.

Efflorescence, a white crystalline or powdery deposit that appears on the surface of brick due to water seepage through the porous surface, can often be removed by scrubbing the dry surface with a stiff-bristle brush and clear water. For tougher deposits, use an efflorescence remover, available at most home centers and hardware stores.

For cleaning brick walkways refer to pages 71 to 73.

PRESTART CHECKLIST:

Tools:
- ✓ Pressure Washer
- ✓ 50 to 100 feet of High-Pressure Hose
- ✓ Cleaning Detergent or Brick Cleaner Formulated for Pressure Washers
- ✓ Brick & Mortar Sealer
- ✓ Eye Protection

Optional
- ✓ Rotating Scrub Brush
- ✓ Stiff-Bristle Brush
- ✓ Efflorescence Remover

Site Prep:
1. Remove any obstacles from the work area.
2. Wet and cover nearby plants and vegetation.
3. Cover nearby electrical components.
4. Close all nearby windows and doors.

CLEANING PERFORMANCE:

Recommended Spray Pattern:

40° Spray Pattern or White Spray Tip

Recommended Distance:

PSI Rating:	Nozzle Distance:
2000 or less	6 in. to 12 in.
2000 to 3000	12 in. to 24 in.
3000 or more	18 in. to 30 in.

1 Prior to pressure washing, patch any damaged mortar joints to prevent water from seeping behind walls. Allow the mortar to dry for at least one week before pressure washing.

2 Adjust the nozzle to high-pressure mode: slide the adjustable nozzle backward and twist to a wide spray pattern, or install the white 40°-spray tip.

3 Standing at a distance to the surface, thoroughly soak the brick with plenty of clear water to help prevent absorption of detergents or cleaners. Work from the bottom of the wall section to the top.

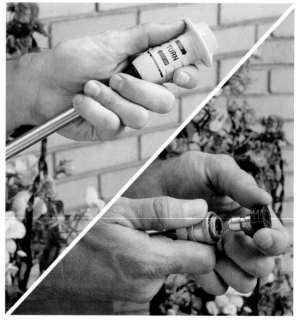

4 Adjust the nozzle to low-pressure mode: slide the adjustable nozzle forward or install the black spray tip. Prepare the cleaning detergent or brick cleaner according to the manufacturer's instructions, and insert the detergent injection tube and filter into the container.

CLEANING PROJECTS

5 *Depress the spray trigger until detergent is present in the water stream, then apply to the surface, working from bottom to top in identifiable sections. Allow detergent to dwell for 5 to 10 minutes (20 minutes for brick cleaners). Do not let detergent dry; rewet as needed.*

VARIATION: *Use a Rotating Scrub Brush attachment to help penetrate heavily soiled areas and scour built-up grime.*

6 *Adjust the nozzle to high-pressure mode: slide the adjustable nozzle backward and twist to a wide spray pattern, or install the white 40°-spray tip. Depress the spray trigger to flush any remaining detergent from the line.*

7 *Test the cleaning power on an inconspicuous area of the surface and make any necessary adjustments (pages 30 to 31). Rinse off detergent residue, working from top to bottom and covering two to three rows of brick with the spray pattern. Move on to the next identifiable section to continue cleaning. After pressure washing, seal brick with a brick & mortar sealer, following the manufacturer's instructions.*

CLEANING PROJECTS

A pressure washer makes short work of cleaning decks and fences. A quick high-pressure spray can remove superficial dirt and grime, while a thorough wash with a pressure washer formulated cleaning detergent will eliminate ground-in stains, saturated oil and sap, and built-up moss and mildew. The various nozzle settings are especially useful for cleaning hard-to-reach corners of a deck railing system or the tight spaces of a picket fence.

Today's decks and fences may be constructed from wood, aluminum, plastic, or composite products—all of which can be safely and efficiently cleaned with the pressure washer, following proper techniques and safety precautions.

When using a cleaning detergent, use only those that are approved for decks and fences. Do not use bleach or bleach-based products—bleach destroys the lignin that holds together wood fibers, removes the natural color of wood, corrodes metal fasteners and hardware, and kills any surrounding vegetation. Bleach can also damage the pressure washer's water pump and detergent injection system.

Pressure Washing Wood

Wood remains the most common building material for decks and fences. Pressure washing can get down to the wood grain, stripping old sealers and paint, or removing the gray discoloration from a neglected, weathered deck or fence. It must be remembered, however, that wood is a relatively soft material; an intense blast of highly pressurized water can damage wood fibers, resulting in a frayed, splintered, or even gouged surface.

Before pressure washing your wood deck or fence, always test the nozzle spray in an inconspicuous area of the work surface and adjust the cleaning power as needed (see pages 30 and 31). Always use wide spray patterns and moderate cleaning power when pressure washing wood—0°-spray patterns will quickly cause damage to wood surfaces.

Note on CCA-Treated Lumber—Decks and fences built from pressure-treated lumber may have been treated with Chromated Copper Arsenate, or CCA. Contact your local or state health department or the Environmental Protection Agency (EPA) for more information and handling procedures.

Pat Simpson:
PRO TIP

When cleaning any surface, start at a distance and move closer until desired effect is achieved.

Restoring a Deck

Pressure washing is the most effective method for cleaning a deck. The high-pressure spray can get down to the wood grain to strip old sealers and paint or remove the gray discoloration of a neglected, weathered deck.

When cleaning a deck built with alternative materials, such as plastic-wood composites, use the same cleaning techniques as for wood. Though these products may be capable of withstanding increased water pressure, always test the high-pressure spray on an inconspicuous area to determine the proper cleaning power.

A deck should have a fresh coat of sealer-preservative or stain every two years to maintain its durability and beauty. Using a pressure washer will help speed up the removal of old, worn layers of finish, providing a fresh, clean surface that allows the new sealer to adhere properly.

PRESTART CHECKLIST:

Tools:

✓ Pressure Washer
✓ Deck & Siding Wash Formulated for Pressure Washers
✓ Deck Sealer-Preservative

✓ Eye Protection

Optional
✓ Floor Brush

Site Prep:

1. Remove any obstacles from the work area.
2. Wet and cover nearby plants and vegetation.
3. Cover nearby electrical components, including outdoor light fixtures.
4. Sweep away any loose debris.
5. Close any nearby windows and doors.

CLEANING PERFORMANCE:

Recommended Spray Pattern:

40° Spray Pattern or White Spray Tip

Recommended Distance:

PSI Rating:	Nozzle Distance:
2000 or less	8 in. to 18 in.
2000 to 3000	12 in. to 24 in.
3000 or more	18 in. to 36 in.

1 *Adjust the nozzle to low-pressure mode: slide the adjustable nozzle forward or install the black spray tip. Prepare the Deck & Siding Wash cleaning detergent according to the manufacturer's instructions, then insert the detergent injection tube and filter into the container.*

2 *Depress the spray trigger until detergent is present in the water stream, then apply to the surface, working in identifiable sections. Allow detergent to dwell for 5 to 10 minutes. Do not let detergent dry; rewet as needed.*

VARIATION: *Use a Floor Brush attachment to help penetrate heavily soiled areas and scour built-up grime.*

3 *For deck railing systems, apply detergent from bottom to top. For more effective cleaning, use a Utility Brush attachment to scrub detergent between rail balusters and in tight corners. Allow detergent to dwell for 5 to 10 minutes. Do not let detergent dry; rewet as needed.*

Restoring a Deck (continued)

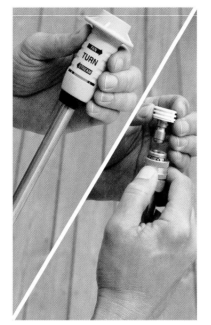

4 *Adjust the nozzle to high-pressure mode: slide the adjustable nozzle backward and twist to a wide spray pattern, or install the white 40°-spray tip. Depress the spray trigger to flush any remaining detergent from the line.*

5 *Test the cleaning power on an inconspicuous area of the surface and make any necessary adjustments (pages 30 to 31). Rinse off detergent residue, covering one to two deck boards with the spray pattern and following the wood grain. When rinsing the railing system, always work from top to bottom. Move on to the next identifiable section to continue cleaning. After pressure washing, seal the deck with sealer-preservative, following the manufacturer's instructions.*

Cleaning Composite Decking

Materials such as plastics and plastic-wood composites *have become popular alternatives to lumber. To clean these materials, follow basic pressure washing techniques (pages 22 to 37) and use Deck & Siding Wash or Multi-Purpose cleaning detergents.*

For faster and more effective cleaning, *use a Floor Brush attachment or a turbo nozzle to pressure wash composite decking.*

Cleaning a Fence

Cleaning a dirty fence or weathered fence is fast and easy with a pressure washer. For best results:

✓ Use a wide fan spray or a 25° or 40° Quick-Change spray tip for high-pressure cleaning.
✓ Use long, even, overlapping strokes, following the grain of the wood. At the end of each stroke, arc slightly up and away from the work surface.
✓ Keep the nozzle spray in motion when it is close to the wood—stopping or pausing can damage the surface.
✓ Keep the spray nozzle 8 to 36 inches from the work surface.

PRESTART CHECKLIST:

Tools:
✓ Pressure Washer
✓ Deck & Siding Wash Formulated for Pressure Washers
✓ Eye Protection

Optional
✓ Floor Brush
✓ Rotating Brush

Site Prep:
1. Remove any obstacles from the work area.
2. Wet and cover nearby plants and vegetation.
3. Cover nearby electrical components, including outdoor light fixtures.

CLEANING PERFORMANCE:
Recommended Spray Pattern:

40° Spray Pattern or White Spray Tip

Recommended Distance:

PSI Rating:	Nozzle Distance:
2000 or less	8 in. to 18 in.
2000 to 3000	12 in. to 24 in.
3000 or more	18 in. to 36 in.

Cleaning a Fence (continued)

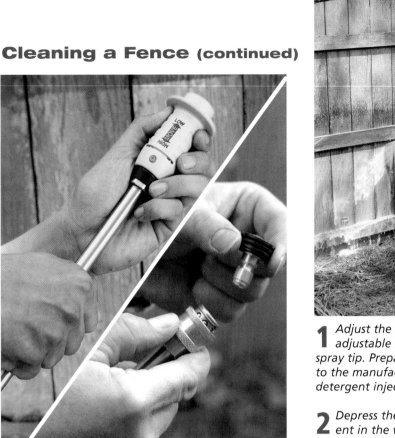

1 *Adjust the nozzle to low-pressure mode: slide the adjustable nozzle forward or install the black spray tip. Prepare the cleaning detergent according to the manufacturer's instructions, and insert the detergent injection tube and filter into the container.*

2 *Depress the spray trigger until detergent is present in the water stream, then apply to the surface, working from bottom to top in identifiable sections. Allow detergent to dwell for 5 to 10 minutes. Do not let detergent dry; rewet as needed.*

VARIATION: *Use a Rotating Scrub Brush attachment to help penetrate heavily soiled areas and scour built-up grime.*

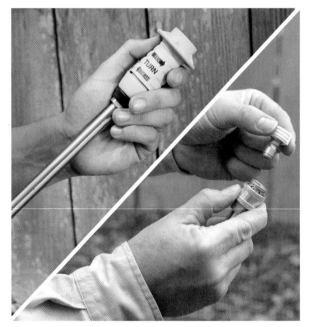

3 *Adjust the nozzle to high-pressure mode: slide the adjustable nozzle backward and twist to a wide spray pattern, or install the white 40°-spray tip. Depress the spray trigger to flush any remaining detergent from the line.*

CLEANING PROJECTS

4 *Test the cleaning power on an inconspicuous area of the surface and make any necessary adjustments (pages 30 to 31). Rinse off detergent residue, working from top to bottom. Cover one to two boards with the spray pattern and follow the* wood grain. Move on to the next identifiable section to continue cleaning. After pressure washing, seal the fence with paint or sealer-preservative, following the manufacturer's instructions.

Other Fence Materials

VINYL / PVC

CHAIN LINK / WROUGHT IRON

A quick high-pressure rinse with a wide spray pattern is often enough to restore vinyl fencing's original, glossy finish. For thicker dirt and grime, treat with Multi-Purpose cleaning detergent prior to rinsing.

A pressure washer will restore the metallic shine to a dull gray chain-link fence. Use a narrow spray pattern, such as a 15° to 25°, to blast away dirt, debris, and unwanted plant-life from the irregular surfaces of chain-link mesh.

Driveways, Sidewalks & Patios

Driveways, walkways, and patios are dealt daily doses of grease, oil, dirt, and salt that get impacted and ground in by foot traffic and vehicles. Though these surfaces are crafted from materials designed to withstand the abuse, they do still stain and soil. Long-standing stains and embedded grime are not only unpleasant sights, they can weaken bonding agents in concrete, brick, and tile, causing the materials to deteriorate prematurely. However, this is where a pressure washer becomes your greatest asset.

A pressure washer is simply the best tool for cleaning concrete, brick, and tile. Because these durable surfaces can withstand a great amount of force, a pressure washer provides safe and extremely effective cleaning. With the aid of a cleaning detergent or degreaser, seemingly permanent stains, such as oil, rust, and efflorescence, can be drastically reduced and even removed.

After you've pressure washed a driveway, walkway, or patio, it should be resealed to help prevent future stains from setting and to keep the outdoor surface looking its best.

Cleaning Concrete

Pressure washing is the most effective method for cleaning concrete driveways, patios, and walkways. Because concrete is quite durable, use narrower spray patterns to intensify the cleaning power for heavily soiled areas, though always start at a distance and move closer to the surface until you achieve the desired results. For stubborn stains, use a Floor Brush attachment or turbo nozzle. These specialty attachments can provide more effective cleaning and better control of the nozzle spray.

Typically, general dirt and grime can be cleaned with a straight high-pressure wash. Stains and marks left by tires, organic materials (grass and leaves), and mild oil deposits can be removed with Multi-Purpose detergent and Heavy-Duty Degreaser. After pressure washing is complete and the concrete has dried for 24 hours, apply a concrete sealer, following the manufacturer's instructions.

PRESTART CHECKLIST:

Tools:

✓ Pressure Washer
✓ Heavy-Duty Degreaser or Multi-Purpose Wash Formulated for Pressure Washers
✓ Concrete Sealer
✓ Eye Protection

Optional
✓ Floor Brush
✓ Turbo Nozzle
✓ Water Broom
✓ Surface Cleaner
✓ Mold & Mildew Remover

Site Prep:

1. Remove any obstacles from the work area.
2. Wet and cover nearby plants and vegetation.
3. Cover nearby electrical components.
4. Sweep away any loose debris.

CLEANING PERFORMANCE:

Recommended Spray Pattern:

40° Spray Pattern or White Spray Tip

Recommended Distance:

PSI Rating:	Nozzle Distance:
2000 or less	4 in. to 10 in.
2000 to 3000	8 in. to 18 in.
3000 or more	12 in. to 30 in.

Cleaning Concrete (continued)

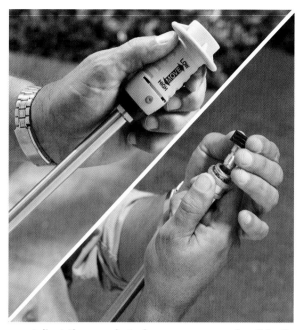

1 *Adjust the nozzle to low-pressure mode: slide the adjustable nozzle forward or install the black spray tip. Prepare the Multi-Purpose detergent or Heavy-Duty Degreaser according to the manufacturer's instructions. Insert the detergent injection tube and filter into the detergent container.*

2 *Depress the spray trigger until detergent is present in the water stream, then apply to the concrete surface, working in identifiable sections and following any slope to promote drainage. Allow detergent to dwell on the surface for 5 to 10 minutes. Do not let detergent dry; rewet as needed.*

VARIATION: *Use a Floor Brush attachment to help penetrate oil and grease deposits and scour heavy grime and stains.*

3 *Adjust the nozzle to high-pressure mode: slide the adjustable nozzle backward and twist to a wide spray pattern, or install the white 40°-spray tip. Depress the spray trigger to flush any remaining detergent from the line.*

CLEANING PROJECTS

4 *Test the cleaning power on an inconspicuous area of the surface and make any necessary adjustments (pages 30 to 31). Rinse off detergent residue, passing over heavily soiled areas multiple times. Move on to the next identifiable section to continue cleaning.*

5 *For faster cleaning, use a turbo nozzle to cut through heavy stains with ease. Always keep the turbo nozzle in motion as you work.*

VARIATION: *Pressure washing works wonders on the irregular surfaces of exposed aggregate, though it is more vulnerable than concrete. Reduce the cleaning power to prevent loosening the embedded stones.*

Pat Simpson:
PRO TIP
CLEANING GARAGE FLOORS

When pressure washing garage floors, make sure to open all garage doors, clear the floor of obstacles, and cover walls, workbenches, and fixed equipment with plastic drop cloths if you do not want them to get wet. To minimize extraneous spray during cleaning, direct the deflected water spray toward the open garage

doors and away from walls and equipment. The pressure washer itself must be operated outdoors.

Follow basic pressure washer operation and techniques *when cleaning asphalt. Always work in identifiable sections and following the slope of the surface to promote drainage. Apply Multi-Purpose detergent with a Floor Brush to help break up heavy stains and deposits, and take multiple passes over the soiled areas when rinsing.*

Use your pressure washer *to "edge" your driveways, sidewalks and patios: adjust the nozzle to a narrow spray pattern, around 25° to 40°, and direct the spray just off the edge of the surface to cut back overgrown lawn. Make sure to direct the intense spray pattern away from buildings, vegetation, and your body.*

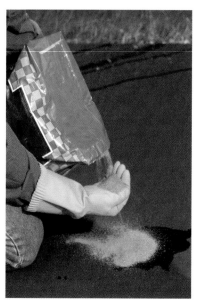

If oil and grease stains remain, *apply an oil absorbent; follow the manufacturer's instructions. Wear protective clothing, rubber gloves, and eye goggles when using harsh solvents, especially acids, and flush the area with plenty of clear water when finished.*

PRESTART CHECKLIST:

Tools & Materials:
✓ Pressure Washer
✓ Multi-Purpose Cleaning Detergent Formulated for Pressure Washers
✓ Eye Protection

Optional
✓ Floor Brush
✓ Oil Absorbent
✓ Asphalt Sealer
✓ Water Broom
✓ Surface Cleaner

Site Preparation:
1. Remove any obstacles from the work area.
2. Wet and cover nearby plants and vegetation.
3. Cover nearby electrical components.
4. Sweep away any loose debris.

Cleaning Asphalt

Asphalt is yet another surface material for which pressure washing is ideal, though heavy oil stains present a particular challenge. Heavy-Duty Degreasers rarely work because asphalt itself consists of varying proportions of crude petroleum. The best approach is to cover stains with cat litter or sawdust to soak up as much oil as possible. Sweep away the debris and pressure wash, spraying over the area repeatedly to break up the stains.

Using a floor brush will also help break up heavy stains and deposits. However, do not use a turbo nozzle on asphalt because the spray pattern produced can damage the surface. If stains remain after pressure washing, apply an oil absorbent, following the manufacturer's instructions. In addition, asphalt should be resealed after pressure washing. Once the asphalt has dried completely (about an hour), apply an asphalt sealer, following the manufacturer's instructions.

CLEANING PERFORMANCE:

Recommended Spray Pattern:

40° Spray Pattern or White Spray Tip

Recommended Distance:

PSI Rating:	Nozzle Distance:
2000 or less	8 in. to 18 in.
2000 to 3000	12 in. to 24 in.
3000 or more	16 in. to 36 in.

CLEANING PROJECTS

Cleaning Brick Patios & Walks

Pressure washing is the best method for brightening dull brick patios and walkways. Typically, using a Multi-Purpose detergent followed by a high-pressure rinse is enough to finish the job. However, heavy stains and mildew buildup will require the use of a brick cleaner or Mold & Mildew Remover detergent. After pressure washing, allow brick to dry for two to three days, then apply a brick sealer, following the manufacturer's instructions.

Because dry brick absorbs liquids, including cleaning detergents, thoroughly presoak the brick prior to applying detergents to prevent discoloration. If efflorescence, a white crystalline or powdery deposit that appears on the surface brick, is a problem, scrub the surface with a stiff-bristle brush and clear water. For tougher deposits, use an efflorescence remover, available at most home centers and hardware stores.

Use caution when cleaning brick patios and walkways with sand-filled joints—pressure washing can force sand out of joints, weakening the entire surface.

PRESTART CHECKLIST:

Tools & Materials:

- ✓ Pressure Washer
- ✓ Cleaning Detergent or Brick Cleaner Formulated for Pressure Washers
- ✓ Eye Protection

Optional
- ✓ Floor Brush
- ✓ Stiff-Bristle Brush
- ✓ Efflorescence Remover
- ✓ Turbo Nozzle
- ✓ Water Broom
- ✓ Surface Cleaner

Site Preparation:

1. Remove any obstacles from the work area.
2. Wet and cover nearby plants and vegetation.
3. Cover nearby electrical components.
4. Sweep away any loose debris.

CLEANING PERFORMANCE:

Recommended Spray Pattern:

40° Spray Pattern or White Spray Tip

Recommended Distance:

PSI Rating:	Nozzle Distance:
2000 or less	6 in. to 12 in.
2000 to 3000	12 in. to 24 in.
3000 or more	18 in. to 30 in.

CLEANING PROJECTS

1 *Adjust the nozzle to high-pressure mode: slide the adjustable nozzle backward and twist to a wide spray pattern, or install the white 40°-spray tip.*

2 *Standing at a distance to the surface, thoroughly soak the brick with plenty of clear water to help prevent absorption of detergents or cleaners.*

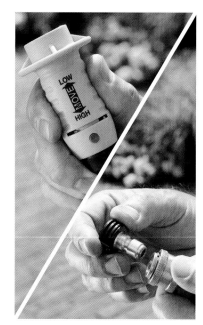

3 *Adjust the nozzle to low-pressure mode: slide the adjustable nozzle forward or install the black spray tip. Prepare the cleaning detergent or brick cleaner according to the manufacturer's instructions, and insert the detergent injection tube and filter into the container.*

4 *Depress the spray trigger until detergent is present in the water stream, then apply to the surface, working in identifiable sections. Allow detergent to dwell for 5 to 10 minutes (20 minutes for brick cleaners). Do not let detergent dry; rewet as needed.*

VARIATION: Use a Floor Brush attachment to help penetrate heavily soiled areas and scour built-up grime.

5 *Adjust the nozzle to high-pressure mode: slide the adjustable nozzle backward and twist to a wide spray pattern, or install the white 40°-spray tip. Depress the spray trigger to flush any remaining detergent from the line.*

6 *Test the cleaning power on an inconspicuous area of the surface and make any necessary adjustments (pages 30 to 31). Rinse off detergent residue, covering two to three rows of brick with the spray pattern. Move on to the next identifiable section to continue cleaning.*

7 *If efflorescence is a problem, scrub the deposits with a stiff brush and clear water. If the staining remains, apply an efflorescence remover, following the manufacturer's instructions. Do not siphon efflorescence remover through the pressure washer's detergent injection system. After application, flush the area with plenty of clear water from a garden hose, then rinse thoroughly with a high-pressure spray from the pressure washer.*

Pat Simpson:
PRO TIP
OUTDOOR TILE

Mold and mildew buildup is a common problem on tile patios. To remove, scrub the surface using a Floor Brush attachment and a Mold & Mildew Remover detergent, then rinse thoroughly using a wide spray pattern. Once the patio dries completely, seal grout lines and tile with exterior-grade sealers, follow the manufacturer's instructions for both applications.

Vehicles & Boats

A pressure washer takes the work out of cleaning vehicles and boats. The spray wand provides excellent control of the water stream, allowing you to easily access all those hard-to-reach places, such as vehicle undersides and wheel wells. The high-pressure water stream can penetrate the many joints, creases, and crevices, significantly cutting detail time. In addition, the use of a soft-bristle, Rotating Scrub Brush attachment will help cut through the traffic film that causes finished surfaces to appear dingy and dull.

When pressure washing a vehicle or boat,

always start with the nozzle at least 4 to 5 feet from the surface and then move closer as needed. Vary the distance as you work to prevent damage to fragile materials and parts, such as plastic light covers, door and window seals, rubber gaskets and hoses, and painted surfaces.

Be particularly careful around chipped or cracked paint—the highly pressurized water is powerful enough to strip paint. Always use a wide-fan spray, and keep the water stream in constant motion. Do not get closer than 6 inches when cleaning tires.

Cleaning a Car or Truck

For effective and efficient cleaning of your car, truck, or other vehicle, first remove thick mud and dirt (especially on the vehicle's underside), then clean oil and grease deposits on the transmission and engine, and finally wash off the light grime, called "traffic film," that soils the bodywork. Use a Multi-Purpose/Vehicle Wash cleaning detergent designed for pressure washing, and follow the manufacturer's instructions for application procedures.

After pressure washing, allow the vehicle to dry completely, then apply a protective coat of polish or wax to preserve the paint surface, following the manufacturer's instructions printed on the container.

PRESTART CHECKLIST:

Tools & Materials:
- ✓ Pressure Washer
- ✓ Multi-Purpose/Vehicle Wash Formulated for Pressure Washers
- ✓ Soft Towel
- ✓ Car Polish or Wax
- ✓ Eye Protection

Optional
- ✓ Rotating Scrub Brush
- ✓ Floor Brush

Site Preparation:
1. Move vehicle to an open area, such as a driveway.
2. Roll up all windows.
3. Remove all items from truck beds.

CLEANING PERFORMANCE:

Recommended Spray Pattern:

40° Spray Pattern or White Spray Tip

Recommended Distance:

PSI Rating:	Nozzle Distance:
2000 or less	18 in. to 24 in.
2000 to 3000	24 in. to 36 in.
3000 or more	30 in. to 48 in.

Cleaning a Car or Truck

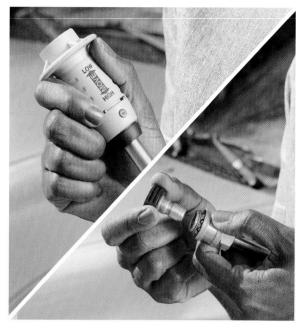

1 Adjust the nozzle to low-pressure mode: slide the adjustable nozzle forward or install the black spray tip. Prepare the Multi-Purpose/Vehicle Wash detergent according to the manufacturer's instructions, and insert the detergent injection tube and filter into the container.

2 Depress the spray trigger until detergent is present in the water stream, then apply to the vehicle, working from bottom to top. Pay close attention around the grill, bumpers, and wheel wells where dirt and mud tend to collect. Allow detergent to dwell on the surface for 5 to 10 minutes. Do not let detergent dry; rewet as need.

VARIATION: Use a Rotating Scrub Brush attachment to help penetrate traffic film and scour built-up grime, insects and grease.

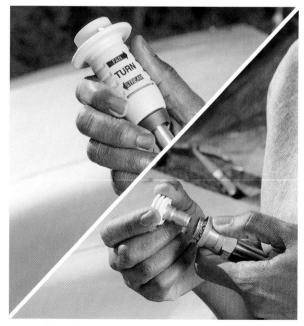

3 Adjust the nozzle to high-pressure mode: slide the adjustable nozzle backward and twist to a wide spray pattern, or install the white 40°-spray tip. Depress the spray trigger to flush any remaining detergent from the line.

CLEANING PROJECTS

4 *Test the cleaning power on an inconspicuous area of the surface and make any necessary adjustments (pages 30 to 31). Rinse off detergent residue, working from top to bottom to avoid streaks. To avoid peeling or removing decals and graphics, hold the nozzle at a 90° angle to the surface, working from the center outward.*

5 *Do not get closer than 6 inches when cleaning tires. To clean truck-bed liners, use a narrow spray pattern to penetrate the textured surface. After pressure washing is complete, hand-dry the vehicle with a soft towel and apply a protective coat of polish or wax to preserve the paint surface.*

Other Vehicle Cleaning Ideas

Degrease an engine *prior to maintenance or repair—disconnect the battery and wrap all electrical components, such as the distributor cap and alternator, with plastic and duct tape. Use extra caution when spraying near seals, gaskets, hoses, belts, and cables, as well as electrical components and plastic casings. When finished, thoroughly spray WD-40 or silicone on all degreased metal parts, components, and electrical connectors to prevent rust and corrosion. Be careful not to directly spray belts or hoses.*

Cleaning ATVs—*Apply Multi-Purpose/Vehicle Wash detergent and rinse with a wide spray pattern. Do not spray directly at electrical components, brake pads and calipers, oil and dust seals, hoses, belts, chains and cables, and keep at least 6 inches away from tires. After the vehicle dries completely, lubricate all metal parts and components with WD-40 or silicone. Also lightly spray all pivots and control linkages (such as throttle levers).*

Cleaning a Boat

Keeping your boat clean will not only increase its life, it also will help stop zebra mussels, Eurasian milfoil, and other invasive aquatic species from spreading from one freshwater lake or river to another.

Pressure washing in lakes, rivers, or other waters is prohibited almost everywhere. Any high-pressure cleaning of boats, hulls, and trailers should be done on a concrete slab where debris and detergent waste can be contained without running back to the shoreline to contaminate waters. After pressure washing, sweep or vacuum the slab and properly dispose of the waste.

Before pressure washing, remove any canvas canopies, removable seat cushions, and equipment from inside the boat. Follow basic pressure washer operation and techniques, pages 22 to 37.

PRESTART CHECKLIST:

Tools:
- ✓ Pressure Washer
- ✓ Multi-Purpose/Vehicle Wash Formulated for Pressure Washers
- ✓ Hull Polish or Boat Wax
- ✓ Eye Protection

Optional
- ✓ Rotating Brush
- ✓ Motor Flusher

Site Prep:
1. Move boat to obstacle-free work area.
2. Cover nearby electrical components.
3. Sweep away any loose debris.

CLEANING PERFORMANCE:
Recommended Spray Pattern:

40° Spray Pattern or White Spray Tip

Recommended Distance:

PSI Rating:	Nozzle Distance:
2000 or less	18 in. to 24 in.
2000 to 3000	24 in. to 36 in.
3000 or more	30 in. to 48 in.

Tips for Cleaning Your Boat

When pressure washing your boat, pay close attention around the motor, trailer rigging, and wheel wells where grime and invasive aquatic species tend to collect. Do not get closer than 6 inches when cleaning trailer tires. Additionally, flush the bilge, live well, and any other equipment exposed to lake or river water liberally with hot soapy water.

For more effective cleaning, apply Multi-Purpose/Vehicle Wash detergent. Use a rotating scrub brush on the hull and body of the boat. After rinsing with a wide spray pattern, allow the boat to dry for two days, then apply a protective coat of hull polish or boat wax, following the manufacturer's instructions.

Flush the outboard motor's cooling system: Connect the garden hose to a motor flusher and attach to the water inlet vents on the motor using manufacturer's instructions. Turn on the water, then start the motor. Water will spray everywhere. A stream of water will also be expelled from the base of the engine as it cycles through the cooling system. If it does not, stop the engine immediately and adjust the motor flusher.

Vinyl seats can also be cleaned with your pressure washer. Remove the seats from the boat and place on a durable surface, such as a driveway. Apply Multi-Purpose/Vehicle Wash detergent using a Rotating Scrub Brush to penetrate heavy grime and stains, then rinse with a wide spray pattern.

Stripping Paint

Stripping paint manually with a scraper or wire brush is a labor-intensive, time-consuming task. But a pressure washer's powerful jet stream can penetrate textured surfaces to lift paint with ease and efficiency, and can significantly cut your workload.

Stripping paint requires a pressure washer with a rather high PSI rating (2500 to 3700 PSI), as well as the use of narrow spray patterns.

Because a more intense water stream is needed, there is an increased risk of damage to the substrate, especially soft wood. Always make sure to test the cleaning power on a small, inconspicuous place to determine the most effective—and least damaging—pressure washer settings.

Stripping Paint from House Siding

Before a house is repainted, all the loose and peeling paint must be removed. This provides a clean surface to which the new coat can properly adhere. However, it is not necessary to strip all the paint from the surface; paint that remains bonded to the siding should be sanded to blend with the rough surface and then painted over. It is also beneficial to lightly sand any glossy or smooth surfaces, such as stripped wood.

If it is necessary to remove all the paint from siding, a chemical paint remover may be required. When using chemical strippers, always follow the manufacturer's instructions, and wear protective clothing, rubber gloves, eye protection, and a tight-fitting ventilation mask. Do not use your pressure washer to apply chemical strippers.

Note on Lead Paint: If you own a home that was built prior to 1978, you will need to contact your local or state health department or the housing and building office for any lead-paint restrictions. Lead is recognized as a hazardous material and many governmental groups restrict lead-paint stripping or require that it be removed professionally.

PRESTART CHECKLIST:

Tools & Materials:
- ✓ Pressure Washer
- ✓ 50 to 100 feet of High-Pressure Hose
- ✓ Landscaping Fabric
- ✓ Paint Scraper
- ✓ Disc Sander
- ✓ 60- to 120-Grit Sandpaper
- ✓ Dust Mask
- ✓ Eye Protection

Site Preparation:
1. Remove any obstacles from the work area.
2. Wet and cover nearby plants and vegetation.
3. Cover nearby electrical components, including light fixtures.
4. Close all nearby windows and doors.

CLEANING PERFORMANCE:

Recommended Spray Pattern:

15° Spray Pattern or Yellow Spray Tip

Recommended Distance:

PSI Rating:	Nozzle Distance:
2000 or less	2 in. to 12 in.
2000 to 3000	4 in. to 18 in.
3000 or more	6 in. to 24 in.

Stripping Paint from House Siding (continued)

1 Cover the ground around the perimeter of the house with landscaping fabric to collect paint chips. For every 15 feet of house height, extend the ground cover from the house by 10 feet.

2 Adjust the nozzle to high-pressure mode: slide the adjustable nozzle backward and twist to a wide spray pattern, or install the white 40°-spray tip.

3 Hold the nozzle at a 45° angle to the surface and test the cleaning power on an inconspicuous area—the nozzle spray should remove loose and peeling paint within a few passes without causing any damage to the substrate.

4 If needed, adjust the nozzle to a narrower spray pattern: twist the adjustable nozzle or install the yellow 15° or red 0°-spray tip. Note: Do not use the pinpoint spray pattern or red 0°-spray tip on wood.

5 As you work, hold the nozzle at a 45° angle to the surface to allow the water stream to get beneath old paint layers. Also, try to spray at a slightly downward angle to help direct paint chips toward the landscaping fabric. Avoid the temptation to remove well-adhered paint—the extra effort potentially can damage the substrate. For a second story or walls over 12 feet, use narrower spray patterns to propel the water stream to the necessary heights.

6 Once pressure stripping is complete, scrape any remaining areas with a paint scraper or wire brush. Sand rough, glossy, or heavy paint spots with fine-grit sandpaper, smoothing the edges between painted and bare areas. When finished, carefully roll up the landscaping fabric and dispose of paint waste properly. Use a wet/dry vacuum to clean up remaining paint chips on the ground. Allow siding to dry at least 24 hours before painting.

Removing Graffiti

A high-pressure blast from a pressure washer can remove unsightly graffiti from most surfaces. Always test the cleaning on a portion of the graffiti: start with a wide spray pattern and low Impact PSI and make slight adjustments until paint starts to come off without causing damage to the substrate.

To remove graffiti on durable surfaces, such as masonry and brick, use a turbo nozzle to enhance cleaning effectiveness and save time.

Swimming Pools & Spas

Swimming pools and outdoor spas collect dust, dirt, and debris that can clog the filtration system and compromise the quality of the water. Algae, the most common pool and spa contaminant, can carry bacteria and cause slipperiness in and around the water area. Adding pressure washing to your maintenance routine will help extend the life of your system equipment, providing you with added years of pool and spa enjoyment.

Pools and spas made from plaster, exposed aggregate, or concrete—typically troweled smooth and then painted or tiled—are ideal candidates for pressure washing. Vinyl-lined and fiberglass pools and spas should not be pressure washed, but instead should be cleaned with chemical treatments and non-abrasive cleaning methods.

Before you can clean your concrete pool or spa, the water must be drained. Check with your local EPA (Environmental Protection Agency) for proper wastewater treatment and disposal regulations. Vinyl-lined and fiberglass pools should not be drained after installation, as the weight of the refill water can cause the liner to buckle and separate from the frame. Always consult the manufacturer's specifications to determine if pressure washing is recommended. Never use an electric pressure washer around any pool area. As always, make sure there is adequate airflow to remove the carbon monoxide gas that emits from any gasoline engines or around any pool area.

Pressure washing is also ideal for maintaining the areas and structures around pools and spas, such as decking, cabanas, and patio furniture. When cleaning around a pool or spa, keep dirt and debris from being sprayed into the water. Do not pressure wash filter cartridges—the high-pressure spray will cause damage to the filter media faces.

Cleaning a Swimming Pool

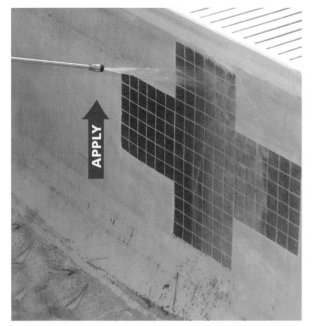

1 *After the pool water has been properly drained, sweep up and dispose of any leaves and debris. Start pressure washing at pool walls, working in manageable sections. Always apply cleaning detergents starting at the bottom of the wall section and work upward. For basic pressure washer operation and cleaning techniques, see pages 22 to 37.*

2 *As you rinse—working from top to bottom— direct the dirt and detergent residue away from the work area. When pressure washing the pool floor, start at the edges and work toward the drain, flushing dirt and residue away from you. For heavy buildup or stains, consider using a turbo nozzle.*

3 *If algae is a problem, it must be properly treated to prevent re-growth. The two most common types of algae, black and yellow (or mustard), both can be removed with a high-pressure rinse followed by a treatment of swimming pool algaecide or a mixture of 1 part bleach to 4 parts water applied by hand using a utility brush.*

4 *Allow the algaecide to soak for 10 minutes, then thoroughly rinse the area in high-pressure mode using plenty of clear water. Other stubborn stains— typically caused by leaves, metal objects, and mineral deposits—can be treated with a Multi-Purpose detergent.*

Lawn & Garden Equipment

Lawn and garden work often requires tools and machinery that move earth, haul waste, or shred debris. Such equipment is built to withstand abuse, but dirt, mud, and grime can still impede performance and cause damage to engine parts. A quick rinse with a pressure washer will help keep your yard and garden equipment running longer and performing efficiently.

Typically, a high-pressure rinse is enough to blast away dry mud and impacted grass and leaves. Detergent usually will not be needed,

but a heavy-duty degreaser may be useful on a small engine prior to maintenance, repair, or storage. (If detergent is used, be sure to choose a product formulated for pressure washers.)

As with any pressure washing project, start at a distance from the cleaning surface, then move closer to increase the cleaning power. Use caution when spraying the engine and body surfaces of machinery, so as not to strip paint, remove warning decals, or damage sensitive engine parts.

Cleaning a Lawn Mower

1 *Disconnect the spark-plug lead prior to cleaning. For added safety, also remove the lawn mower blade. Start pressure washing by rinsing out the bottom of the mower deck, removing impacted grass and debris. Do not get closer than 6 inches when spraying rubber tires. If needed, use a Multi-Purpose detergent to treat heavy buildup.*

2 *Once the underside is clean, set the mower upright and rinse off heavy residue and buildup from the discharge shoot and the top of the mower. After the unit is completely dry, reconnect the spark-plug lead and spray any exposed metal surfaces with WD-40 or silicone to prevent rust and corrosion.*

Other Lawn & Garden Equipment Cleaning Ideas

Pat Simpson:
PRO TIP
CLEANING GARDEN TOOLS

A pressure washer's high-pressure spray makes cleaning lawn and garden tools quick and easy. To remove thick and impacted mud from shovels, pitchforks, wheelbarrows, or other non-sensitive metal surfaces, thoroughly spray the tools and let soak for a few minutes, then rinse with a high-pressure, tight-fan spray.

To clean garden tillers, *as well as other lawn and garden equipment, such as cultivators, edgers, chipper/shredders, and snow throwers, use a high-pressure rinse to eliminate built-up dirt and grime, and help prevent premature engine or machinery failure. Make sure to spray any exposed metal surfaces with WD-40 or silicone to prevent rust and corrosion after pressure washing.*

Outdoor Furniture & Accessories

Through general use, winter storage, or simply weather, outdoor furniture and accessories can collect plenty of dirt, grease, and grime. A wash and rinse from a pressure washer can quickly revitalize furniture, barbecue grills, and other outdoor accessories for another season of enjoyment.

A high-pressure blast is often all it takes to clean surface dust and dirt from furniture frames and vinyl-covered seat cushions. Stubborn stains in cushions should be spot cleaned, then rinsed with plenty of clear water

to flush out any detergent from inside the material. Extremely soiled or stained items, such as barbecue grills, will require treatment with a Multi-Purpose cleaner or Heavy-Duty Degreaser, followed by a high-pressure rinse.

In addition to its use in general cleaning, a pressure washer is handy in furniture restoration: use a high-pressure setting and tight-fan spray to help strip paint from a weathered wood bench or help remove rust from a neglected wrought-iron chair. (See "Stripping Paint" on pages 80 to 83.)

Cleaning Outdoor Furniture

Outdoor furniture is crafted from a wide variety of materials, including wood, wrought iron, aluminum, vinyl, and plastics. Each of these materials can be safely cleaned with a pressure washer, but caution must be taken to prevent damage to each material's particular finished surface. For best results when cleaning any furniture surface, always begin with a wide spray pattern at a distance; then move closer as needed to increase the effective cleaning power. A turbo nozzle can be used on wrought-iron and vinyl furniture frames.

To avoid unwanted cleaning of surrounding areas, clean your outdoor furniture on an open, durable surface, such as a driveway or patio. Remove all seat cushions from chairs and benches, and umbrellas from tables, prior to pressure washing.

Use a high-pressure, wide spray pattern to remove general dirt and grime from furniture frames. Use a Multi-Purpose detergent and a Brush attachment to treat and penetrate heavy buildup and stubborn stains.

To clean vinyl-covered seat cushions, reattach the cushions to the furniture frame to hold them in place, then rinse thoroughly in high-pressure mode. Spot clean stubborn stains by hand using a utility brush and hot soapy water, followed by a high-pressure rinse with plenty of clear water to flush any detergent from inside the cushion.

The restoration of old patio furniture can go faster with your pressure washer. A tight spray pattern will strip old paint and finishes with ease, leaving you very little sanding and scraping work. However, use caution when stripping wood; concentrated blasts of water, such as that produced by the 0° spray pattern, can damage wood fibers.

Cleaning a Barbecue Grill

Pat Simpson:
PRO TIP

CLEANING GRILL GRATES

Pressure washing is a fast and effective method for removing the built-up grease and grime that accumulates on a barbecue grill over a summer of outdoor cooking. The following tips are applicable to both charcoal and gas grills, though you need to make sure to disconnect the propane tank from a gas grill prior to pressure washing.

To keep your grill clean between uses, lightly spray the grates with non-stick oil prior to cooking. After grilling is done and the fire is out—but the grill is still warm—clean the grates with a wire brush. Once the grill has cooled, be sure to clean up any spills. Always keep the hood closed when the grill is not in use.

When cleaning grill grates, move them to a driveway or other durable surface. Apply a Heavy-Duty Degreaser detergent and let dwell for 10 to 15 minutes. For heavy buildup, use a Utility Brush attachment to help scour between the grating. When rinsing, use a narrow spray pattern, such as a 15°, 25°, or turbo nozzle, to penetrate heavy grease deposits. Once the grates have dried completely, coat with a non-stick oil.

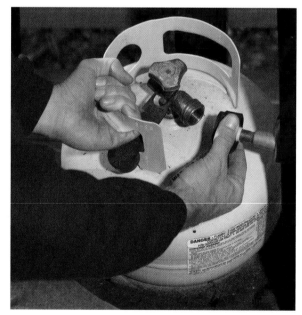

1 *Prop up grill hood securely, and remove grates. For gas grills, disconnect the propane tank and set aside, away from the work area. Start with an application of Heavy-Duty Degreaser detergent, working from the bottom of the cart upward to the grill bed. Use caution when spraying near or around gas hoses, electrical wiring, and heating elements.*

2 *After the degreaser has set for a few minutes, thoroughly rinse off the residue using a wide spray pattern. On gas grills, also check the briquettes or lava rocks. If they are greasy, apply degreaser and rinse thoroughly with a wide spray pattern. Allow the grill to dry, then reattach the propane tank.*

Other Outdoor Accessory Cleaning Ideas

Pressure washing is ideal for cleaning a neglected birdbath, however the best and safest approach is to use plain, clear water—detergents and cleaners can potentially harm birds and other wildlife. Use a Rotating Scrub Brush or Utility Brush attachment for heavily soiled areas. If mold or algae are a problem, scrub by hand using a mild bleach solution and a stiff-bristle brush. Rinse well with plenty of clear water, using a wide spray pattern. Return birdbath to its usual location, and refill with fresh water.

Plant containers will benefit from a high-pressure rinse to remove impacted dirt and grime. Start at a distance and move closer to clear imbedded debris in decorative ridges and detailing.

General dust and dirt can be removed with a quick blast from your pressure washer. Use a wide spray pattern at a distance to prevent chipping or removing paint from surfaces.

Other Surfaces & Uses

In addition to the numerous applications discussed throughout this book, there are many other surfaces and structures around your home that can benefit from pressure washing. Arbors and gazebos can be prepped for a new coat of paint or sealer-preservative. Landscape ponds and masonry fire pits can be cleaned for off-season shutdown. And there are countless pressure washing opportunities around a hobby farm, such as cleaning heavy equipment or animal trailers.

Pages 93 to 95 offer a number of additional uses for your pressure washer. Follow basic operation and cleaning techniques when pressure washing any surface or structure (see pages 22 to 37).

BEFORE BEGINNING ANY PRESSURE WASHER PROJECT:
✓ Clear the area of any obstacles and cover nearby plants and electrical components.
✓ Test the high-pressure spray on an inconspicuous area to determine the appropriate pressure settings (pages 30 and 31).
✓ Choose cleaning detergents that are pressure-washer safe and biodegradable.
✓ Make sure the unit is on stable ground.
✓ Wear eye protection.

Cleaning Garbage Cans

1 *Pressure washing garbage cans will eliminate the debris and odors that attract insects and stray animals. Apply a Multi-Purpose cleaning detergent using a Rotating Scrub Brush to help cut through grime and stop odors. For tough stains and particularly strong odors, use a solution of 1 part bleach to 4 parts water and scrub by hand.*

2 *When rinsing, anchor the garbage can against a solid object, such as a garage or fence, to prevent it from moving under the powerful nozzle spray. Stand off to the side when rinsing the interior of the can to avoid being hit with deflected dirty water and debris. Rotate the can to rinse all interior surfaces. When done, turn the garbage can upside down, and let dry completely.*

Cleaning Mini-Blinds

1 *Although not an outdoor structure or surface, mini-blinds are a perfect candidate for pressure washing. Prior to cleaning, hang the blinds outside by fastening the top arm to a clothesline pole, the swing beam of a play structure, or hooks mounted on a fence or garage wall, and tying down the bottom arm to the ground. Pull the blind all the way down and close the slats.*

2 *When pressure washing, use a wide spray pattern held at least 24 inches from the surface to prevent damage to the slats and pulley system. Apply a diluted Multi-Purpose cleaning detergent from bottom to top and rinse away the residue from top to bottom. After both sides are cleaned, untie the blinds from the hanging system, then pull the unit tight and set on one end to dry before re-hanging.*

Other Pressure Washing Ideas

Arbors provide light shade *and add visual interest to your landscape, but constant exposure to sun, rain, and harsh weather can leave these structures looking less than desirable. A high-pressure rinse from your pressure washer will quickly restore the wood's natural beauty or help strip old paint for a fresh coat and new appearance.*

Children love their play structures *and toys. Unfortunately, so do dirt, grime, and germs, which are easily transferred to little hands and faces. Using a pressure washer to clean play structures can help keep children healthy and enjoying their outdoor playtime.*

Clean and sanitary kennels *are a key factor in raising healthy dogs. Contaminated pens—as well as insect, parasite, or rodent infestations—can make pets sick. Pressure washing is the fastest and most effective method for keeping your dog's home clean.*

An attractive business *or storefront will attract the attention of potential customers and new clientele. A pressure washer is ideal for keeping signs readable, awnings clean, and entranceways inviting.*

Keeping expensive commercial and industrial machinery clean and functioning is the concern of every company owner. Pressure washing tools and equipment will help extend each unit's operation life, increase access to bolts and connectors, and prevent contamination of parts during maintenance and repair.

Heavy-equipment operators already know the benefits of pressure washers—they have been using them to remove impacted dirt and grime and keep their machinery performing at its best for many years. No matter how big the outdoor cleaning project, the best tool for the job is a pressure washer.

Pat Simpson:
PRO TIP

EVEN MORE PRESSURE WASHING IDEAS

Along with the wide variety of projects presented in this book, you also can use your pressure washer to clean:

✓ Trellises
✓ Wrought Iron
✓ Indoor/Outdoor
   Carpeting
✓ Boardwalks
✓ Docks
✓ Retaining Walls
✓ Porches
✓ Sheds
✓ Fire Pits

✓ Garden Ponds
✓ Snowmobiles
✓ RVs
✓ Tractors
✓ Canoes
✓ And much, much
   more!

MAINTENANCE & STORAGE

Following a regular maintenance schedule will help keep your pressure washer performing at its peak for years to come. General engine and water pump maintenance, such as changing the oil and cleaning or replacing the spark plug and air filter, should be made at least once each season, or more frequently if the unit is used often or under dusty or dirty conditions. In addition, filter screens and connectors should be cleaned and checked periodically to ensure the unit is performing at its peak.

Proper maintenance also includes preparing your pressure washer for storage. Careful treatment of the engine and pump prior to long-term storage will keep sensitive parts lubricated and prevent mineral deposits and damage from freezing temperatures. Always store your pressure washer in a cool, dry place.

Most manufacturer warranties do not cover items that have been subject to operator abuse or negligence. To ensure your warranty remains valid, set good maintenance habits when your pressure washer is new, and always consult the owner's manual for special guidelines for your pressure washer make and model.

Preventative Maintenance

Taking the time to examine and clean your pressure washer and accessories, both before and after each use, will help you avoid performance problems and save money on parts and repair. Refer to your owner's manual for special guidelines appropriate to your pressure washer make and model.

PRIOR TO EACH USE:

✓ Check engine oil and fuel levels: Top off both oil and fuel if low, or change oil if needed, using a manufacturer-recommended oil. Consult engine's owner's manual for instructions.

✓ Check inflatable tires: Keep air pressure at value marked on tires or within 15 and 25 PSI.

✓ Check water inlet screen: Flush with clear water if dirty or clogged; replace with new screen and rubber washer if damaged (page 101).

✓ Check in-line screen: Flush with clear water if dirty or clogged; replace with new screen and O-ring if damaged (page 101).

✓ Inspect high-pressure hose: Replace if leaks, cuts, abrasions, or bulging of cover exists or if couplings are damaged or have movement. New hoses must exceed maximum pressure rating of your pressure washer.

✓ Examine cleaning detergent injection tube and filter: Clean if dirty or clogged (page 36). Examine tube for leaks or tears; make sure it fits tightly on barbed fitting. Replace tube or siphon/filter if either is damaged.

✓ Test spray wand assembly: Replace O-rings if connectors leak (page 100). Clean nozzle orifices if clogged (page 102), or replace spray wand, adjustable nozzle, or spray tips if original parts are damaged.

✓ Rinse out garden hose: Flush debris from hose prior to attaching to pump inlet.

AFTER EACH USE:

✓ Flush the cleaning detergent injection system: Run clean water through the system for two minutes before stopping the engine.
✓ Shut down the pressure washer: Shut off engine and let cool. Turn off water supply.
✓ Relieve the pressure in the system: Press and hold spray-gun trigger until all water remaining in the line is expelled. Disconnect high-pressure and garden hoses from pump, and detach high-pressure hose from spray gun.
✓ Empty pump of remaining liquids: Pull the recoil handle six times. A small amount of water will leak from the pump's water outlet.

Replacing O-Rings & Screens

O-rings keep the spray wand and hose connections tight and leak free, while screens help prevent debris from clogging hoses and damaging the water pump. Through normal operation of the pressure washer, these parts may become clogged, worn, or damaged and should be cleaned or replaced before the unit is operated.

Some manufacturers include a maintenance kit with the unit that contains replacement O-rings, rubber washers, screen filters, and a wire tool for cleaning nozzles. Maintenance kits can also be obtained at most home centers.

REPLACING O-RINGS

To replace an O-ring, use a small flathead screwdriver to pry off the worn or damaged O-ring and discard. Install an O-ring in the same position as the old one.

CLEANING & REPLACING WATER INLET SCREEN

1 Use a small flathead screwdriver to remove the inlet screen from the hose connector. If the screen is clogged, flush it and the hose connector with clean water. If the screen is damaged, replace it with a new one with the dome-side of the screen pointed outward.

CLEANING & REPLACING IN-LINE SCREEN

1 Detach the high-pressure hose and wand from the spray gun. Remove the O-ring and in-line screen from the wand extension. Flush the screen, spray gun, and wand with clean water from a garden hose to clear debris.

2 If the screen is damaged, replace it with a new one: Place a new screen into the threaded end of the wand, pushing it in with the eraser end of a pencil until it rests flat at the bottom of the opening. Be careful to not bend the screen. Place a new O-ring into the recess, pushing it snugly against the screen. Reattach the wand to the spray gun.

Spray Wand Maintenance

1 *Shut off the engine and turn off the water supply. Depress the spray-gun trigger to relieve the pressure in the system. Detach the wand from the spray gun. If you have an adjustable nozzle, twist the nozzle to STREAM, then remove the nozzle orifice using a 2mm (or 5/64) Allen wrench. If you have Quick-Connect spray tips, simply remove the spray tip from the nozzle.*

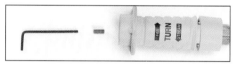

Prior to use, always test the spray gun to make sure it works properly. To begin, make sure the hose connection to the spray gun is secure, then test the spray-gun assembly by pressing and releasing the trigger—the trigger should spring back into place when it is released. Next, engage the safety latch, and test the trigger— you should not be able to depress it. If the trigger is loose, or can be depressed while the safety latch is engaged, or water is leaking around the gun handle, the spray gun should be replaced immediately.

A pulsing sensation felt while squeezing the spray-gun trigger might be due to excessive pump pressure, typically the result of a clogged or restricted nozzle. If this occurs, immediately clean the nozzle and wand filter.

2 *Use a paper clip to free any foreign material clogging or restricting the orifice or spray tip (inset). Note: Some manufacturers provide a wire nozzle-cleaning tool with the maintenance kit.*

3 *Flush water through the nozzle for one minute to remove debris. For an adjustable nozzle, turn the nozzle to STREAM and move from low- to high-pressure mode while flushing. Reinstall the orifice into the adjustable nozzle (do not overtighten), or install the spray tip into the nozzle, then reconnect the wand to the spray gun and test to ensure the nozzle works properly.*

Water Pump Maintenance

PURGING THE PUMP OF CONTAMINANTS

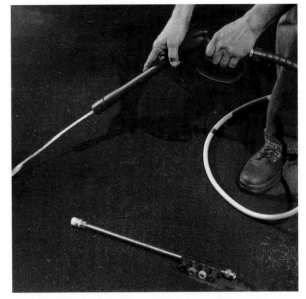

Pressure washer water pumps need relatively low maintenance. The two main concerns are keeping contaminants out of the pump and changing the pump oil on schedule. (Some pumps do not need oil changes.) Purge the water pump to remove impurities and debris and change the pump oil every 50 hours of use or once a year, whichever occurs first. Use only oil recommended by the manufacturer, as specified in the owner's manual. (Purchase premeasured bottles of pump oil for water pumps without dipsticks.) Never use special oil additives or detergents, unless specified in the owner's manual.

If you do not plan to use your pressure washer for more than 30 days, refer to "Winterizing & Storage" on page 105.

***Prepare the pressure washer for use** (pages 26 to 27). Turn on the supply water, then remove the wand from the spray gun. Start the engine, then squeeze and hold the spray-gun trigger until there is a constant, steady stream of water. Hold for 2 minutes, then engage the trigger safety latch, and refasten the wand to the spray gun.*

CHANGING PUMP OIL

1 *Drain the oil and fuel from the engine. Remove the oil cap on the water pump with an Allen wrench. Tilt the pressure washer to drain the used oil into an approved container. Tilt the unit back in the opposite direction after the oil has drained.*

2 *Fill the water pump with fresh oil, following the directions in the owner's manual. Note: Premeasured bottles of water pump oil are available for some models. Reinstall the oil cap and tighten firmly, then wipe up any excess oil around the cap and set the pressure washer in the upright position. Clean up any spilled oil, and dispose of used oil and soiled rags in accordance with local environmental statutes.*

Engine Maintenance

Proper engine maintenance will help your pressure washer run better and last longer. Manufacturers recommend changing the engine oil after every 25 hours of use. Once a year, you should also clean or replace the spark plug and air filter to ensure proper fuel-air mixture.

Performing your own tune-up is a simple 4-step process. You'll find everything you need for a tune-up plus easy-to-follow instructions in each Briggs & Stratton small engine maintenance kit, available at home centers and hardware stores nationwide. Refer to your engine's owner's manual for instructions on proper engine maintenance. Use only manufacturer-approved parts and supplies.

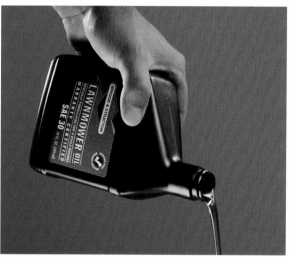

Changing Oil: Changing the oil keeps the engine properly lubricated and ensures clean oil is continuously distributed to critical engine components, reducing friction. Less friction results in less wear and tear on engine components.

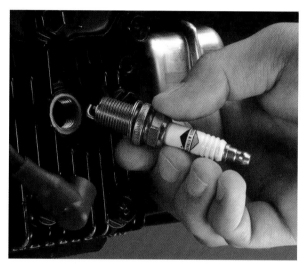

Spark Plug: An eroded or fouled spark plug provides an inconsistent spark. Replacing the spark plug each spring ensures a consistent spark, making starting more reliable and improving fuel economy.

Air Filter: Changing the air filter prevents clogging. A clogged air filter reduces the air/fuel ratio, resulting in higher fuel consumption. The lower air/fuel ratio also leads to excess or unburned gasoline, resulting in the release of extra hydrocarbons. Hydrocarbons form ground-level ozone, a major component of smog.

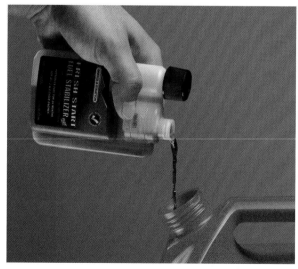

Fuel Stabilizer: Fuel stabilizer improves starting by preventing stored gasoline from degrading to the point where it is no longer combustible.

Winterizing & Storage

Typically, pressure washers are used seasonally, then sit idle for long periods. Long-term storage can aggravate overlooked problems, and allow other problems to develop. For example, unstabilized gas left in an engine can gum up the carburetor, unlubricated engine parts can corrode, and moisture can accumulate in the ignition system. With proper storage preparation, you can avoid most problems. For instruction on proper engine storage, see the opposite page and consult the owner's manual.

Additionally, water should not remain in the water pump or hoses for long periods of time.

Sediments or minerals can deposit on pump parts and "freeze" pump action. Prior to long-term storage, clean and empty the water pump and hoses. (See "After Each Use," page 100.)

If your pressure washer will not be used for more than 30 days or will be stored over the winter, treat the water pump with an antifreeze product such as Briggs & Stratton's PumpSaver™, which is designed to prevent freeze damage, lubricate pistons and seals, and protect against mineral deposits. Failure to treat the water pump can cause premature pump failure.

Pat Simpson:
PRO TIP

ACCESSORY ATTACHMENT MAINTENANCE

As with the rest of your pressure washer, your accessory attachments must also be cared for to ensure their ongoing performance. After each use, and before long-term storage, make sure to:

✓ Flush any brush attachment or turbo nozzle extensions with plenty of clean, clear water.
✓ Flush and scrub brush bristles to remove debris and waste.
✓ Flush the turbo nozzle head with clear water to remove debris.

To use Briggs & Stratton's PumpSaver™, read and follow all instructions on the container. Make sure the pump is emptied of all remaining liquid. Always wear eye protection when using PumpSaver™.

With maintenance complete, store your pressure washer and accessories in a cool, dry place.

Troubleshooting Guide

Pressure washer repairs should always start with troubleshooting—the search for the source of a problem—starting with the most obvious or simple explanation and working toward the less obvious or more complex.

When troubleshooting a pressure washer problem, you need to rule out the various parts or systems as possible sources of the problem. It's important to work systematically to isolate the cause rather than skipping parts or systems that you believe are in good working order.

FOR SUCCESSFUL TROUBLESHOOTING:
✓ Make sure you consider all symptoms carefully.
✓ Look for the cause, not just the cure for the symptoms.
✓ Gather as much information as possible.

Remember that a simple solution is not always the correct one, or may be only a partial solution. Replacing worn O-rings and filter screens may cure leaky connectors and help maintain pressure in the system, but the real culprit may be a faulty water pump. In this case, the problem will probably turn up again soon.

When troubleshooting small engine malfunctions, always refer to the engine's owner's manual. You can also consult Briggs & Stratton's *Small Engine Care & Repair* for all your small engine maintenance and repair needs.

If this is the problem:	Ask this question:	If the answer is yes:
Pump fails to produce pressure, has erratic pressure, or has a loss of pressure or low water volume.	*Is the engine running at full speed?*	Move the throttle control to the FAST position.
	Is the nozzle in low-pressure mode?	Pull the adjustable nozzle back for high-pressure mode, or install a high-pressure spray tip (page 29).
	Is the inlet/garden hose kinked or leaking?	Straighten the garden hose, or patch the leak.
	Is the water inlet blocked or water-inlet filter screen clogged or damaged?	Disconnect the garden hose from the water inlet; clean the water inlet and filter screen. If screen is damaged, remove damaged screen, insert new screen (page 101).
	Is the high-pressure hose blocked or damaged?	Disconnect the high-pressure hose, and clear blockages from the hose line. If damaged, replace hose with a new one rated higher than the maximum PSI rating of your pressure washer.
	Is the high-pressure hose leaking?	Check the O-rings. If damaged, pry off old O-ring with a small, flathead screwdriver, and replace with new one (page 100).
	Is the in-line filter screen clogged or damaged?	Disconnect the high-pressure hose from the spray gun; remove the in-line filter screen; clean by flushing with clear water. If damaged, replace filter and O-ring (page 101).
	Is the spray gun leaking?	Replace the spray gun with a new one.
	Is the nozzle orifice obstructed?	Shut off the engine; purge air from the pump; remove the orifice from the adjustable nozzle or remove the spray tip from the nozzle extension; clean the orifice or spray tip using the wire tool from the maintenance kit (page 102).
	Is the supply water temperature over 100°F?	Provide a cooler water supply.
	Is the supply water pressure and flow rate adequate? (Supplying a minimum of 20 PSI and 1 GPM more than the GPM rating of the unit?)	Test the supply water using a pressure/flow-rate gauge. If the supply water does not produce a minimum of 20 PSI and 3.5 GPM, provide an adequate water supply.
	Is the pump oil level low?	Add oil to the pump (page 103).
	Is the pump faulty?	Contact Briggs & Stratton service facility.
	Is the nozzle in high-pressure mode?	Push the adjustable nozzle forward for low-pressure mode, or install the low-pressure (black) spray tip (page 29).

If this is the problem:	Ask this question:	If the answer is yes:
Detergent fails to mix with nozzle spray.	*Has the cleaning detergent tube come out of the detergent bottle?*	Insert the cleaning detergent tube into the detergent (page 34).
	Is the cleaning detergent siphon/filter clogged or cracked?	Clean or replace the siphon/filter.
	Is the cleaning detergent tube dirty, clogged, or damaged?	Place the injection siphon/filter in clear water; adjust nozzle to low-pressure mode; depress nozzle for 2-3 minutes. If damaged, replace with a new one (page 36).
	Is the in-line filter screen dirty, clogged, or damaged?	Disconnect the high-pressure hose from the spray gun; remove the in-line filter screen, and flush with clear water to clean. If damaged, replace filter and O-ring (page 101).
	Is the nozzle in low-pressure mode?	The nozzle must be in low-pressure mode for the detergent injection system to work.

Shopper's Guide

When servicing and repairing your pressure washer use original engine manufacturer's replacement parts and supplies available from authorized service dealers and outdoor power equipment retailers. Quality replacement parts and supplies will make a difference in how well your pressure washer performs after maintenance and repair.

When you shop for replacement parts, take along both your pressure washer and engine model numbers and a list of the parts you need. You'll save time and avoid repeat trips to the dealer. Also take along any parts you have removed from your pressure washer. They often help an authorized service dealer identify the right parts for your make and model.

To locate an authorized Briggs & Stratton pressure washer service dealer near you, call our toll-free Service Locator system at 1-877-544-0982, or logon to: **www.briggspowerproducts.com**, and click on the "Service" link. There are over 3000 authorized parts and service outlets throughout North America.

(Note: Briggs & Stratton does not offer parts online; all parts must be purchased through an authorized service dealer.)

To find Briggs & Stratton support and service for your pressure washer engine, consult the Yellow Pages under "Engines-Gasoline," "Gasoline-Engines," "Lawn Mowers" or similar categories. You can also contact **Briggs & Stratton Customer Service** by phone at **1-800-233-3723**, or on the Internet at **www.briggsandstratton.com**. There are over 30,000 Briggs & Stratton authorized engine service dealers worldwide who provide quality service.

In addition, you can find Briggs & Stratton pressure washer products, accessories and supplies at major home centers and outdoor power equipment retailers throughout North America.

Resources

Briggs & Stratton Corporation
12301 W. Wirth St.
Wauwatosa, WI 53222
414-259-5333
www.briggsandstratton.com

**Briggs & Stratton Power Products
  Group, LLC**
900 North Parkway
Jefferson, WI 53549
920-674-3750
www.briggspowerproducts.com

ASSOCIATIONS

Power Washers of North America (PWNA)
703-971-4011
800-393-7962
www.pwna.org

**Pressure Washer Manufacturers' Association
  (PWMA)**
1300 Sumner Ave.
Cleveland, OH 44115-2851
216-241-7333
www.pwma.org

**Cleaning Equipment Trade Association
  (CETA)**
7691 Central Avenue NE, Suite 201
Fridley, MN 55432-3541
763-786-9200
800-441-0111
www.ceta.org

PUBLICATIONS

Cleaner Times Magazine
800-525-7038
www.cleanertimes.com

Power Washer's Guide Book (4th revision)
Advantage Publishing Company, Inc.
1000 Nix Road
Little Rock, AR 72211-3235
800-525-7038

HEALTH & SAFETY

U.S. Environmental Protection Agency
Ariel Rios Building
1200 Pennsylvania Avenue N.W.
Washington, DC 20460
202-272-0167
www.epa.gov

National Lead Information Center
422 South Clinton Avenue
Rochester, NY 14620
800-424-LEAD (5323)
www.epa.gov/lead/nlic.htm

CCA Lumber Information:
www.epa.gov/pesticides/factsheets/chemicals/
cca_transition.htm

TECHNICAL INFORMATION—ARTICLES

"The Physics Of Pressure Washing"
By Mike Pearson
www.paintstore.com/archives/pressure-
wash/41.html

"Pressure Washer Reference Area"
By Gary Weidner
http://home.mchsi.com/~gweidner/site

Index